Eyewitness
BASEBALL

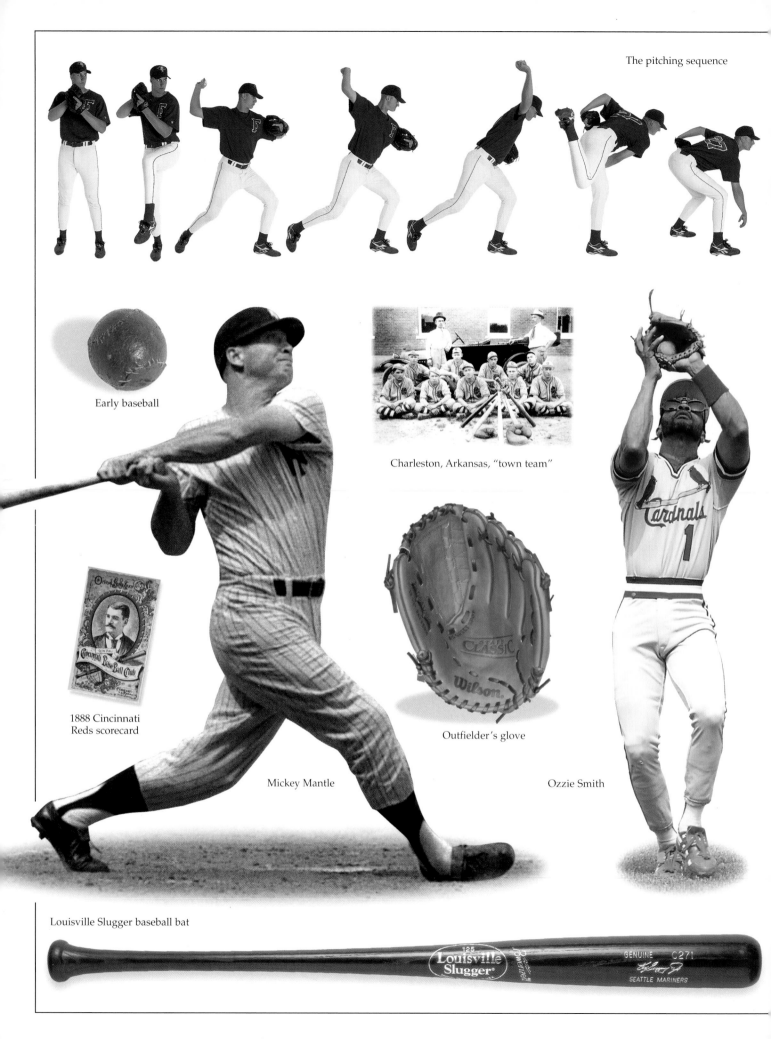

The pitching sequence

Early baseball

Charleston, Arkansas, "town team"

1888 Cincinnati
Reds scorecard

Outfielder's glove

Mickey Mantle

Ozzie Smith

Louisville Slugger baseball bat

Eyewitness
BASEBALL

Written by
JAMES KELLEY

Ted Williams's spikes

Home plate collision

1999 Little League World Series Champions

Babe Ruth and Lou Gehrig

Biography of Satchel Paige

George Brett's Hall of Fame plaque

DK Publishing, Inc.

Eric Gagne

Publisher Neal Porter
Executive Editor Iris Rosoff
Art Director Dirk Kaufman

A Production of the Shoreline Publishing Group
Editorial Director James Buckley, Jr.
Eyewitness Baseball **Designer** Thomas J. Carling
Studio and Memorabilia Photography
Michael Burr and David Spindel

REVISED EDITION
Editors Elizabeth Hester, James Buckley, Jr.
Publishing director Beth Sutinis
Designers Jessica Lasher, Thomas J. Carling
Art director Dirk Kaufman
DTP designer Milos Orlovic
Production Chris Avgherinos, Ivor Parker

This edition published in the United States in 2005
by DK Publishing, Inc.
375 Hudson Street, New York, NY 10014

05 06 07 08 09 10 9 8 7 6 5 4 3 2 1

Women's pro
baseball in
the 1940s

Library of Congress Cataloging-in-Publication Data

Kelley, James
    Baseball / by James Kelley — 1st American ed.
        p. cm.
    Summary: Text and detailed photographs present the
history, techniques, and interesting facts of baseball.
    ISBN 0-7566-1061-3 (hc)   ISBN 0-7566-1062-1 (lib bdg)
    1. Baseball — Juvenile literature [1. Baseball] I. Title Series
(Dorling Kindersley Eyewitness Books)

GV867.5 B83 2000   99-044318
796.357 2I—de21

Original color reproduction by Mullis Morgan, UK
Color reproduction for revised edition by Colourscan, Singapore
Printed in China by Toppan Printing Co.,
(Shenzhen) Ltd.

World Series trophy

1920s
Cleveland
Indians
warm-up
sweater

Discover more at
www.dk.com

Barry Bonds

Contents

Base Ball Beginnings

A BALL, A BAT, AND FOUR BASES ON A FIELD. The elements of the game that became baseball have been around for hundreds of years, most famously in an English game called "rounders." Americans had been playing another ball game with bases called "town ball" since after the Revolutionary War. By the 1840s, sportsmen in several Northeastern cities were gathering regularly to play several variations of what they called "base ball." In 1845, Alexander Cartwright (inset) and Daniel "Doc" Adams, leaders of the Knickerbocker Base Ball Club, developed the first set of rules for the game. Though those rules changed rapidly over the next few years and continued to evolve into the 1900s, they were close enough to what baseball is today to mark the "birth" of baseball. From humble beginnings, the game has grown from a sport played by gentlemen on weekends to a sport played by men, women, boys and girls of all ages in more than 100 countries.

After going west for the California Gold Rush of 1849, Cartwright later became a fire chief in Honolulu

Diamond and base paths

The author's great-grandfather Nicholas Minden

BATTER UP!
From the beginning of the game, baseball bats have maintained their unique shape: thick at the top and tapering to a narrower handle. Early bats did not have as much tapering as today's bats, but their function was the same: "Meet the ball and hit 'em where they ain't."

Thick handle

Union Army uniform

THE DOUBLEDAY MYTH
A 1911 commission to trace the "official" origin of baseball somehow settled on the story of Union Army General Abner Doubleday, who, it was claimed, invented the game in 1839 in Cooperstown, New York. Modern research has completely debunked this theory, although the "myth" of his involvement remains popular today.

TOWN TEAMS
A key to the growth of baseball across America in the late 1800s was the formation of "town teams," such as this one from Charleston, Arkansas (shown before World War I). The players were amateurs, the sponsors local businessmen, and the prize was bragging rights over neighboring towns. But many great players got their start on teams like this one.

BASEBALL HEADS SOUTH
The Civil War (1861-65) helped spread baseball around the country, as Union soldiers took their game, most popular around New York, on the road with them. This noted 1863 lithograph shows Union prisoners at a Confederate camp in Salisbury, North Carolina, putting on a game watched by guards and fellow prisoners alike.

Pitcher

Batter

Catcher

CASEY AT THE BAT

(This is an excerpt from the most famous baseball poem, written in 1888 by Ernest L. Thayer. It tells the story of a fabled player getting one last chance to save the day.)

…Then from 5,000 throats and more there rose a lusty yell;
It rumbled through the valley, it rattled in the dell;
It knocked upon the mountain and recoiled upon the flat,
For Casey, mighty Casey, was advancing to the bat.

There was ease in Casey's manner as he stepped into his place;
There was pride in Casey's bearing and a smile on Casey's face.
And when, responding to the cheers, he lightly doffed his hat,
No stranger in the crowd could doubt 'twas Casey at the bat….

[Several stanzas later…]
…The sneer is gone from Casey's lip, his teeth are clenched in hate;
He pounds with cruel violence his bat upon the plate.
And now the pitcher holds the ball, and now he lets it go,
And now the air is shattered by the force of Casey's blow.

Oh, somewhere in this favored land the sun is shining bright;
The band is playing somewhere, and somewhere hearts are light,
And somewhere men are laughing, and somewhere children shout;
But there is no joy in Mudville — mighty Casey has struck out.

PLAY BALL!
The fist baseballs quickly became soft and mushy as play went on. Players soon learned that winding yarn more tightly around a rubber center, then covering with tightly stitched leather, made a harder ball that traveled farther and lasted longer.

Leather stitching

BASEBALL TUNES
Even bandleader John Philip Sousa (right, in suit) sponsored a team. This song, the "Three Strikes Two-Step," was written in honor of his team. It was one of many tunes, poems (left), and stories about baseball, as it quickly became the "National Pastime."

Birth of the Pros

T HOUGH BASEBALL'S BEGINNINGS WERE HUMBLE, it didn't take long for players to realize there was a way to make money playing this game. By the years after the Civil War, top players were being lured from club to club by secret payments. In 1869, the Cincinnati Red Stockings dropped the pretense and announced themselves as professional players. They barnstormed the East, playing (and defeating) all comers. Two years later, the National Association joined together several pro teams to form the first pro league. From then on, baseball would have two worlds: professional and everyone lese. In the late 19th century, several pro leagues rose and fell. By 1901, there were two established "major leagues," along with several other "minor" pro leagues, much as it is today.

SPALDING'S SPORT
Albert G. Spalding was a top-notch pitcher in his youth, posting an amazing 57-5 record in 1875. He also helped create the National League in 1976, later was the president of the Chicago White Sox, and headed a world baseball tour in 1888. He also founded the still thriving Spalding Sporting Goods Company.

High-button shoes worn for photo, not for games

PRE-WORLD SERIES
The World Series would not begin until 1903, but teams saw the benefit of postseason tournaments early on. From 1894-97, the first- and second-place teams in the National League played each other for the Temple Cup. In 1896 (right), the Baltimore Orioles finished first in the league, and also won the Cup with four straight victories over Cleveland.

Championship medal

EARLY CHAMPS
The Baltimore Base Ball Club won the 1894 National League championship. Playing a style of baseball known as "little ball," they were led by the famously fierce player/manager John McGraw.

EARLY OUTFITS
Early pro players enjoyed snappy outfits as much as today's players do. This heavy wool warm-up sweater was sported by members of the Cleveland Indians, an early entry in the American League.

Thick ribbed wool

FOR THE FANS
The growth of pro teams, such as the American Association's Cincinnati Reds (featuring 27-14 pitcher Lee Viau in 1888, below), led to the creation of numerous scorecards, programs, magazines, and souvenirs fans used to follow their new favorite teams and players.

TAKE ME OUT TO THE BALL GAME

(Written in 1908 by Jack Norworth and Albert Von Tilzer, this song is sung at every baseball game during the top and bottom of the seventh inning—the seventh-inning stretch.)

Take me out to the ball game,
Take me out with the crowd.
Buy me some peanuts and Cracker Jack,
I don't care if I never get back.

So it's root, root, root for the home team.
If they don't win, it's a shame!
For it's one, two, three strikes you're out,
At the Old Ball Game!

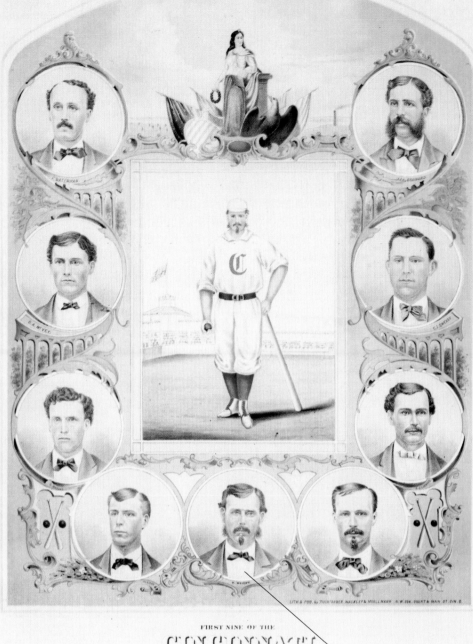

Filed July 31 1869

FIRST NINE OF THE
CINCINNATI
(RED STOCKINGS) BASE BALL CLUB.

Harry Wright

THE FIRST PROS
Harry Wright, captain and founder of the 1869 Cincinnati Red Stockings (left), the first all-professional team, has been called the "father of pro baseball." Along with starting the Red Stockings, Wright invented the basic baseball uniform still used today and patented the first scorecard. He guided his team to an 18-month winning streak, and later led Boston's entry in the new National Association, in 1871.

Note spelling of "Base Ball"

ON THE ROAD
By the turn of the century, pro baseball had spreak as far west as Chicago and St. Louis and as far south as Louisville. This schedule (above) from 1899 also shows the Reds making stops in Washington, Philadelphia, New York, and "Pittsburg," as it was spelled then.

FINALLY...SAFETY
Early catchers wore little or no safety equipment. Spurred by pro players, the first catcher's masks were developed in the 1870s. This model is from near the turn of the century. It would not be until the years before World War I that catchers regularly began using chest protectors and shin guards.

Iron bars

Padded leather

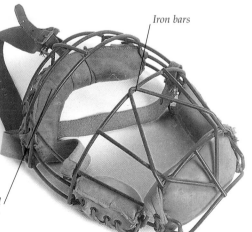

Webbing was simple leather thong.

Early padded first baseman's glove

GLOVES ON FIRST
First basemen were the first noncatchers to use gloves regularly. Having to catch numerous hard throws throughout a game led to the development of this thickly padded mitt. Its flimsy "webbing" was a far cry from today's big, basketlike gloves.

The Babe

WHAT MIGHT HAVE BEEN
With Boston from 1914-19, young Babe Ruth was one of baseball's best pitchers. But Red Sox owner Harry Frazee sold Ruth to the New York Yankees in 1919, forever saddling the Bosox with the "Curse of the Bambino."

WITHOUT QUESTION, George Herman "Babe" Ruth is the most famous and important baseball player in history. It would be hard to overestimate the impact the Babe had on the game, both as a player and symbol. His numbers are "Ruthian," a word that today still conjures up both the might of his sweeping swing and his larger-than-life personality. In 22 seasons (1914-35), The Sultan of Swat slugged 714 home runs. To put that in context, the previous career record holder had 138. When he hit 54 home runs for the Yankees in 1920, his total was more than nearly every other team, and 25 more than the previous record—set by the Bambino himself in 1919. His best single-season total—60 home runs in 1927— was a record for 34 years. Every home run hitter—and every world-famous athlete in any sport—competes with the legend of the Babe. It is a battle they can't win.

Ruth used an unusually large 42-ounce bat.

Officially listed at 215 pounds, Ruth often weighed much more.

A POWERFUL PAIR
Ruth and Lou Gehrig (right) were teammates on the Yankees for 13 years, helping New York win four World Series. Here they are shown in uniforms worn during an off-season exhibition tour. Gehrig was nearly Ruth's equal as a slugger. His career was cut short by the illness that today bears his name.

"Larrupin'" was slang for "slugging."

BUSTIN' BABES

ARRUPIN' LOU'S

Ruth first got number three because he batted third. Uniform numbers weren't used regularly until the 1920s.

Babe Ruth Pays No Tax On His Size
He Is A Giant in Physique, Still His Royal Clothes Cost Nothing Extra On That Account

AN ADVERTISING BABE
Ruth's incredible popularity led to his earning big money (at the time) for endorsements such as this one for large-size men's clothes.

THE "CALLED SHOT"
This statuette of Ruth, showing his famous number 3, recalls one of baseball's most controversial moments. In the 1932 World Series, did Ruth point to the centerfield bleachers right before he slugged a homer there? Or was he waving at the heckling by Cubs' players?

Note the high socks: the style of the times.

BASEBALL'S MIGHTIEST SWING

Ruth incredibly quick wrists and powerful upper body helped him hit 714 home runs. But he was more than simply a home run hitter; Ruth's lifetime batting average of .342 ranks ninth all time.

A baby-faced Ruth got his famous nickname in the minors.

"BABE, SIGN MY BALL"

Some experts believe that Ruth may have signed more autographs than any other sports legend of his day, and certainly more than any today. He signed so many baseballs, bats, programs, and other memorabilia that his signature is not as valuable as other, more reticent stars. He signed this ball the year he died.

BABE ON THE BASEPATHS

Ruth was not the fleetest of runners. In fact, he was thrown out on an attempted steal of a second base to end the 1926 World Series. However, his high on-base percentage and outstanding teammates helped him score 2,174 runs (including this one in 1926), tied for second-most all-time.

BABE AND HIS BABY

Ruth's daughter Dorothy shared her dad with the kids of the world. Raised in an orphanage, Ruth always had a special place in his heart for his youngest fans.

Umpire using classic outside chest protector and mask.

Both players used Louisville Slugger bats.

RECORD SMASHERS

When Mark McGwire and Sammy Sosa rewrote the single-season home run record in 1998, they were toppling records set by these bats. On the bottom, the bat and ball used by Ruth to hit his then-record 60th home run in 1927. In 1961, Roger Maris of the Yankees broke Ruth's record with his 61st home run, using the bat and ball at the top. In '98, McGwire raised the bar first set by Ruth and later toppled by Maris to 70 home runs.

Player signature burned into wood

THE END

In one of baseball's most memorable and poignant photographs, Babe Ruth bids good-bye to fans at his beloved Yankee Stadium—still known today as "The House that Ruth Built"—weeks before his death from throat cancer in 1948. Using a bat for a cane, he thanked his fans and paid homage to the sport he played like no one else.

Ruth had thin legs and famously small feet for a man his size.

The Major Leagues

Arizona
Diamondbacks

Atlanta Braves

Chicago Cubs

Cincinnati Reds

Colorado
Rockies

Florida Marlins

Houston Astros

Los Angeles
Dodgers

Milwaukee
Brewers

American League

Anaheim Angels

THE BEST BASEBALL IN THE world is played by the 30 teams that make up Major League Baseball. The Majors have two parts: the 16-team National League, formed in 1876, and the 14-team American League, which started to play in 1901. Several A.L. teams, including the Boston Red Sox, Detroit Tigers, Chicago White Sox, and Cleveland Indians, remain in the cities they first played in. The Chicago Cubs and Cincinnati Reds survive from the earliest days of the N.L. Over the decades, many teams have moved to different cities, taken on new nicknames, or been added to the Majors. Today, Major League teams are found from coast to coast. One team, the Toronto Blue Jays, plays in Canada. Wherever they play, the teams play the best baseball in the world.

CLASSIC CARDINAL
First baseman Albert Pujols finished in the top four of the National League MVP voting in each of his first three seasons (2001–2003), a first in baseball history. His 114 homers in those three seasons tied a Major League record, too. Pujols combines power (more than 30 homers each season) with batting skill; he was also the 2003 N.L batting champion.

ROCKET MAN
Today's fans are lucky enough to watch some of the greatest players in the history of baseball. Houston Astros' pitcher Roger Clemens is one example. "The Rocket" makes every list of the top pitchers ever. Clemens has won seven Cy Young Awards (with Boston, New York, Toronto, and Houston), more than any other pitcher. He has more than 300 victories in his career and helped the Yankees win two World Series.

FUN FOR THE FANS
While a Major League Baseball game is a great show on the field, many teams add to the entertainment for fans with promotions, giveaways, and mascots, such as Philadelphia's "Phillie Phanatic" (left). And the coolest way to get a souvenir is to catch a foul ball hit into the stands (above).

New York Mets

Philadelphia Phillies

Pittsburgh Pirates

St. Louis Cardinals ▶

Baltimore Orioles

Boston Red Sox

Chicago White Sox

Cleveland Indians

Detroit Tigers

Kansas City Royals

Minnesota Twins

New York Yankees

Oakland Athletics

Seattle Mariners

Tampa Bay Devil Rays

Texas Rangers

Toronto Blue Jays

San Diego Padres   San Francisco Giants

BARRY BASHES FOR THE BOOKS

Fifty years from now, fans of today will look back on Barry Bonds the way fans of yesteryear remember Babe Ruth (see page 10). With an unprecedented show of batting power and skill, Bonds has rewritten the record books and cemented his place among the game's all-time greats. In 2002, he set a single-season record with 73 homers. In 2004, he became only the third player ever to reach 700 career homers (the others are Hank Aaron and Ruth). Bonds is baseball's only seven-time MVP. He also has more than 500 stolen bases and has won eight Gold Gloves. What records are next? Stay tuned!

ROLL ON, RIPKEN

Baltimore's Cal Ripken, Jr., was a throwback hero. In 1996 he played in his 2,131st consecutive game, breaking Lou Gehrig's record. This scorecard is from the final game in Ripken's streak, which ended on September 20, 1998, at 2,632 games. Ripken continued to play but not every day. In 1999, he started his seventeenth straight All-Star Game. He retired in 2001.

VLAD THE POWERFUL

No one is supposed to hit mammoth home runs off of pitches that cross home plate near their ankles. But Vladimir Guerrero has never seen a pitch he could not hit a long way. With Montreal, he was among the N.L.'s best all-around players, combining a powerful bat with a cannon for a right arm. Few baserunners will take a chance on an extra base on Guerrero from right field. In 2004, Guerrero joined the Anaheim Angels and quickly became an A.L. star; he was among league leaders in home runs and RBI.

Guerrero wears his baseball pants the old-fashioned way, showing the whole calf.

Bonds, like many players today, wears full-length baseball pants.

13

The Diamond

IF BASEBALL DIAMONDS WERE ANY OTHER SIZE, baseball probably wouldn't work. But a baseball diamond is exactly 90 feet on each side—that is, the distance between the bases is 90 feet. So each ground ball to shortstop means a close play at first. Each double play is turned in the nick of time. And the time it takes a base stealer to go from first to second is just about the time it takes a pitcher to pitch and a catcher to throw down to second. Of course, a purist might note that a baseball diamond is actually a square viewed from one corner. But the shape is close enough that, at first, the infield area came to be called a diamond; soon, the entire field itself was known by this name. Beyond the base paths is the dirt infield area. The outfield beyond this, the grass (or artificial turf) outfield area. The outfields fences define the back of the field, while the foul lines extending from home plate define the sides. A diamond is much more than lines, fences, and bases, however. A baseball diamond is the place where dreams come true.

DIAMONDS OF OLD
This photo of Griffith Stadium from 1933 shows that diamonds haven't changed much from earlier times. A wide dirt area separated the infield grass from the outfield grass. This view also shows the netting that ballparks put up behind home plate to protect fans from fast-moving foul balls or wild pitches.

Outfield fences, usually padded

Left field

Outfield bleachers

FAIR OR FOUL?
At the outfield end of the two foul lines are tall "foul poles." Any ball hit to the field side of the pole is fair; a ball to the outside of the pole is foul. Any ball that hits the foul pole is, ironically, fair. Most foul poles have nets (below) attached to the field side of the pole to help umpires make their calls.

Left field foul line

Third base

Third base coach's box

ON THE DIAMOND
The geometry of baseball and the diamond on which it is played makes the game unique. The white foul lines stretch out into the outfield, while imaginary lines define the paths between first, second, and third bases. Many teams cut their outfield grass in geometric patterns to create a more pleasing picture for audiences watching both at the park and at home on television.

A BALL CLUB'S SECOND HOME

The area where baseball teams sit during games when they're not on the field is called the dugout. Normally, dugouts are located at or below the level of the playing surface. Players wait on the bench for their turn to bat or rest between innings in the field. In the dugout, players also get refreshments, discuss strategy with their coaches, and cheer on their teammates. In most stadiums, the dugouts lead directly to the locker rooms, where teams dress before the game and shower afterward.

PATH TO THE PLATE

This photo from the 1930s shows two things now only rarely seen on diamonds and at ballparks: a dirt path between the pitcher's mound and home plate (today only Arizona's Bank One Ballpark has this old-time look) and obstructed-view seats. Fans unfortunate enough to sit behind the steel beam upright (center) would have a hard time seeing some plays. Modern stadiums are all constructed without such obstructions.

AT THE CENTER

At the center of every diamond's infield is the pitcher's mound. Rules call for it to be 18 feet in diameter and 10 inches above the level of home plate. The 24-by-6-inch pitching rubber is exactly 60 feet, 6 inches from home plate. A pitcher must be touching the rubber to begin each pitch.

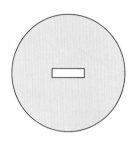

Center field

Second base

Right field

Warning track, made of dirt so outfielders can tell with their feet if they're approaching the wall.

Right field foul line

First base coach's box

First base

Coaches hit pregame warm-up grounders from these "fungo" circles.

Home plate area, including batter's and catcher's boxes

15

Bats and Balls

Take a stick, the lumber, a wand, or a toothpick. Combine it with a pearl, an apple, a pill, a rock, or a pea. What have you got? Everything you need to play baseball. Baseball bats and baseballs have earned many nicknames in the 150 years since the game began to become popular. And while many things have changed, the idea of hitting a round ball with a long, rounded stick has remained the same. The bats and balls used by Major League stars over the years also have become more than just the tools of their trade—they have become the stuff of legend, collected and treasured by generations of fans. Bats used by great players live in the Baseball Hall of Fame. Signed baseballs reside by the thousands on the shelves of fans around the world. And the ball that Mark McGwire hit for his 70th home run in 1998 sold to a private collector for $3 million. A pearl of great price, you might say.

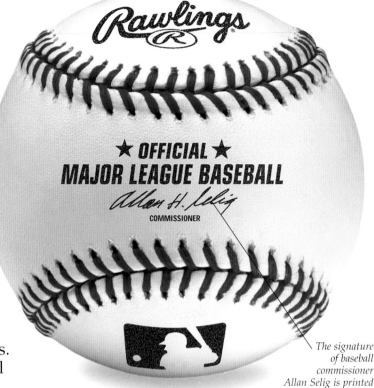

The signature of baseball commissioner Allan Selig is printed on the ball.

WHAT THE PROS USE

Since 1975, the American and National Leagues have used this cow-leather-covered ball made by Rawlings. Before then, the ball was sometimes covered with horsehide and made by Spalding. Home teams must supply five dozen new balls for each regular season game. Umpires or clubhouse personnel "rub them up" with a special compound to erase factory shine.

FROM TREE TO BAT

The most famous model of wood bat used in the Majors is the Louisville Slugger, made by the Hillerich & Bradsby Company in Louisville, Kentucky. To make a bat, first, a Northern white ash tree, at least sixty years old, is cut down. Trees less than 12 inches in diameter are cut into long pieces ("split"). From the center of the split, the "square" is ripsawed. On a lathe, the square becomes a round cylinder. On another lathe, the bat is roughly shaped (note the extra pieces on the ends that hold the bat in place). In the next stage, the bat is sanded smooth. The finished product (below) has been dipped in black lacquer (not all bats are dipped) and then foil branded with the company's famous logo as well as the player's signature.

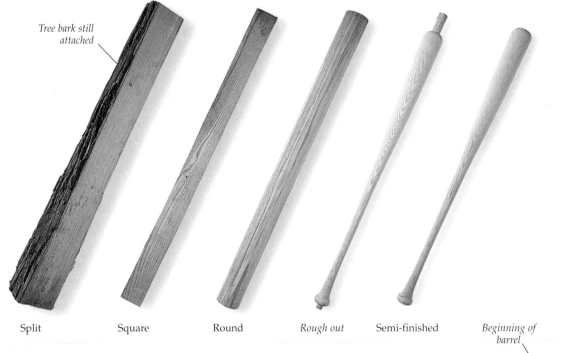

Tree bark still attached

Split   Square   Round   *Rough out*   Semi-finished   *Beginning of barrel*

Knob

Handle

INSIDE THE BASEBALL

Not every baseball is made like this one, but this is the baseball used at the highest level of play in the world: the Major Leagues. Official balls must weigh between 5 and 5 1/4 ounces. They must have a circumference of between 9 and 9 1/4 inches. The lifespan of a Major League baseball during a game is about six pitches. Home team personnel supply new balls as needed to the home plate umpire to put into play.

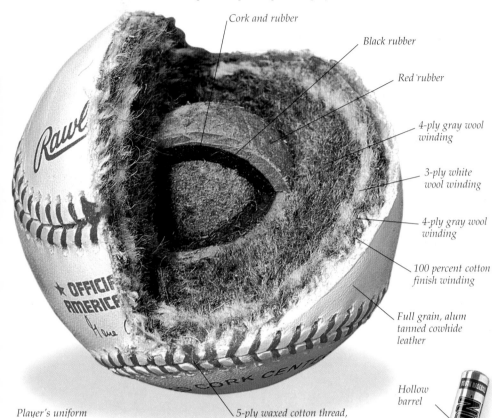

Cork and rubber

Black rubber

Red rubber

4-ply gray wool winding

3-ply white wool winding

4-ply gray wool winding

100 percent cotton finish winding

Full grain, alum tanned cowhide leather

5-ply waxed cotton thread, hand-stitched

THE BOTTLE BAT
The only player to successfully use this strange form of a bat—thinner at the handle and uniformly wide along the barrel, instead of tapering as normal bats do—was Heinie Groh, who played for the Cincinnati Reds from 1912-21.

Player's uniform number

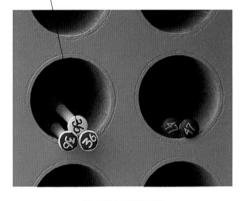

AT THE BAT RACK
Baseball players take good care of their most important offensive tool: their bat. During the game, players store several bats in the bat rack in the dugout. A player might have half a dozen bats at the ready, in case one breaks during a game. Before the season, players get large shipments of bats made to their personal specifications; more can be ordered if necessary.

Hollow barrel

IT GOES PING
The development of the aluminum bat in the early 1970s changed baseball at every level except the professional. Much sturdier than wood bats, aluminum bats last much longer and are almost impossible to break. Youth leagues, high schools, and colleges learned to love the cost efficiency of the aluminum bat. Purists bemoan its odd sound, and the effect aluminum has on batters. What would be simple outs with wood are singles with aluminum; what would be fly outs with wood turn into home runs. Still, more players today use aluminum than wood.

Signature of Ken Griffey, Jr. H&B has thousands of cards on file with the bat preferences of Major Leaguers.

BALLPARK DONUTS
While warming up before hitting, some players slip this weighted ring, called a "donut," onto their bat. It fits over the knob but not the barrel. Swinging the bat with this added weight makes swinging the bat without it seem easier and quicker.

Baseball Gloves

WHILE MANY THINGS ABOUT BASEBALL HAVE REMAINED nearly the same since the first games were played, one piece of equipment—the baseball glove—has undergone many changes. In fact (left), gloves were not even used regularly by players until the late 1800s. Even then, only the catcher wore one, and it was not much more than a leather glove with a bit of padding in the palm. Gloves, or mitts, as they are also called, evolved slowly as more players began using them. The fingers were stitched together. The space between the thumb and forefinger was widened, creating a basket or pocket. The fingers got longer, the better to snare line drives. The leather got looser and more pliable, making the glove more comfortable, and mitts became more specialized for each position. No matter how big or wide or high-tech a baseball glove is, it is only as useful as the hand that is inside it. A glove won't catch a ball all by itself.

Webbing

Pocket

Thumb

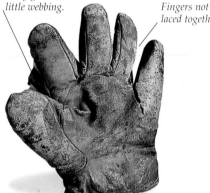

Early gloves had little webbing.

Fingers not laced together

IN THE OLD DAYS
Early gloves, such as this one from the 1920s, offered players little padding compared to today's gloves, and virtually no additional reach. Instead of snagging the ball in the web between the thumb and forefinger, as players usually do today, players back then had to grasp the ball to their palm with their fingers to catch it, rather than cradling it in the webbing.

KIDS' MITTS
Mitts for younger players are the same style as those for major leaguers, except they are smaller. Players young and old use their mitts to field grounders, as this infielder demonstrates. The glove's lacing and webbing create a wide "scoop" that makes this task easier.

JUST LIKE MICKEY
Major League players have long endorsed mitts, whether a replica of the model they use themselves or a kid-sized souvenir model like this one from the 1960s. Note the differences between the earlier model (above left) and this one, with the fingers stitched together, and much wider webbing between thumb and forefinger. Even so, the fingers were still not much bigger than on the hand.

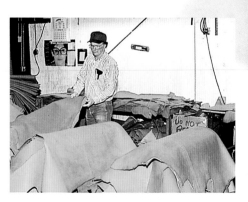

*Laces holding
fingers together*

*Laces holding pieces
of glove together*

GOLD GLOVES
Since 1957, Major League players who excel with their gloves (and their throwing arms) are awarded the Gold Glove (left). There is one winner for each position in each league (three outfielders are chosen in each league). Giants center fielder Willie Mays earned 12 consecutive Gold Gloves, including this one, from 1957-68.

CATCHER'S MITT
Among the most specialized of baseball gloves are those used by catchers. Features include extra padding in the pocket, an extra-wide webbing (right), and an adjustable strap to insure a tight and comfortable fit. This particular glove is made with two colors of leather. Some choose to use one color, usually brown or black.

Model name

PITCHER'S GLOVE
A key to a pitcher's glove is secrecy. Pitchers use their gloves to hide until the last minute the grip they are using on the ball, so they don't give hitters any clue as to what they're throwing. While some outfielders' gloves have open webbing, pitchers always use gloves with closed webbing.

Finger sleeve

BIG SWEET SPOT

STAFF
CLASSIC

Wilson®

Heel

BIG BASKET AT FIRST
After the catcher's glove, the first baseman's glove is the most unique. These gloves are longer and thinner than outfield gloves. They are more pointed at the top, the better to scoop low throws out of the dirt or to stretch out for throws that are off-line. First basemen learn to make catches that create an audible "pop" when the ball hits the mitt. Umpires often listen for the sound while watching the base for the runner's foot.

GLOVE STORY
This typical outfielder's glove shows many of the features that make today's gloves so much better than baseball's first mitts. The large, secure webbing between the thumb and forefinger helps trap the ball; it is where most of the catches are made. The longer fingers help players reach for balls hit or thrown to the side or over their heads. Padding in the heel and in the fingers helps cushion hard-hit balls. And specially chosen leather (left) makes each glove a soft an cushiony basket for making great catches.

Hats and Helmets

Crown

THEY ARE CALLED BASEBALL CAPS, BUT GOLFERS WEAR THEM ON THE GOLF COURSE, race car drivers wear them after races, and football quarterbacks and coaches wear them on the sidelines. And these days, it seems as if everyone in the nonsports world wears them, too. Baseball caps are the game's most important contribution to fashion. While baseball players wear caps for team identity and to keep the sun out of their eyes, many other sports have adopted the distinctive crown and bill of a baseball cap for use in their own sports. Major League players wear very durable, high quality hats fitted to each player's head. When you're in the big leagues, you don't have to deal with those plastic clips at the back of your cap. As for baseball helmets, they are a much more recent addition to the game. While a few players tried some form of helmet in the game's early years, it was only after the development of hard plastic during World War II that a durable and comfortable helmet could be made. Today, baseball players at all levels must wear helmets to protect their heads while batting.

Hard plastic, usually in team color

Ear hole

EXTRA PROTECTION
Many youth leagues now insist that batters wear face guards such as this one along with plastic batting helmets with ear flaps on both sides. Face guards are designed to protect a batter's face from both pitches and foul tips, while also allowing good visibility. Although they can be awkward and uncomfortable, they also can be very helpful, especially to inexperienced players looking for confidence at the plate.

CHANGING TIMES
Just as styles in fashion change through time, so, too, do caps change in baseball. While a few teams have left their cap styles unchanged, these Baltimore Orioles' caps show how teams change colors, logos, and design through the years. In addition, this is a great way to sell more souvenir caps, as fans try to keep up with their heroes.

Team logo patch

EARLY MAJOR LEAGUE HELMETS
The first helmets used in the major leagues were little more than hard plastic versions of the baseball cap, as modeled here by Minnesota Twins slugger Harmon Killebrew (573 carreer home runs). These helmets had little padding and afforded little protection.

Orioles' logo

SAFETY ON TOP

Although plastic batting helmets have been around since the 1950s, it was only in 1971 that wearing them became mandatory in the Major Leagues. Pro players can wear models with only one ear flap (facing the pitcher), while players at other levels wear helmets with two ear flaps. The reason for batting helmets is simple: Being hit in the head with a pitch can be very dangerous. Many players' careers have been shortened after such "beanballs," as they are called. Only one Major League player has died as a result of being "beaned"—Ray Chapman in 1920. Today's players are well-protected.

Strap attached rubber device to cap.

Brim

AN UNPOPULAR FIRST TRY

Players in early baseball didn't have the advantage of plastic. One enterprising company tried marketing this air-filled rubber bladder as a helmet. It attached to the player's cap with an elastic strap. It was ineffective and didn't catch on.

A MOST TRADITIONAL TOPPER

No matter at what level a player plays, from the earliest tee-ball leagues to the Majors, he or she wears a baseball cap on the field. Baseball caps are as much about tradition as function. They keep the sun out of a player's eyes, but what do they do at night? Or in an indoor stadium? Wearing the traditional cap is as much a part of being a ballplayer as swinging a bat. Caps normally are made of six triangular panels held together by a fabric-covered, galvanized steel button at the top. The team logo is on the front of the cap.

Foam padding

Snap for chin strap, sometimes used in youth baseball.

Ventilation holes

FROM THE OLD DAYS

This New York Giants' cap from 1922 shows how baseball caps have changed only slightly over the years. The primary changes have come in the height of the crown and the width of the bill. Early caps were worn more snugly on the top of the head, while bills were a bit shorter.

Brim, usually fabric stitched over heavy cardboard.

Uniforms

THE MAIN REASON FOR UNIFORMS IS SIMPLE—to tell who is on what team. Baseball uniforms are designed to allow freedom of movement and comfort as the player plays the game. Mimicking the first uniforms, today's consists of a short-sleeved shirt (often worn over a longer-sleeved undershirt), pants with a belt, and a baseball cap. Now, baseball uniforms are made of tight-fitting, stretchy polyester and other synthetic fabrics. Early uniforms were made of heavy wool that got heavier as the game wore on and the player sweated. Then and now, baseball pants are unique in sports. They are supposed to stop just below the knee, as they did until the last decade. But today's fashion-conscious Major Leaguers, however, almost always prefer much longer pants, even while bucking tradition. Unfortunately, these long pants hide another unique part of the baseball uniform: stirrup socks worn over white socks. As with any baseball equipment, the uniform is not as important as what the player does while he's wearing it.

Fitted cap

Year made (1952), size (46), player's number (9)

SUPERSTAR SHIRT AND SHOES
Each team has a unique design on its jerseys. This home Red Sox jersey belonged to the great Ted Williams. Boston has not changed its basic logo for decades, but other teams have changed their looks and logos several times. Williams's baseball shoes (below) show that the basic configuration of the metal spikes (three-pronged triangles at front and back) has not changed much since the "Splendid Splinter" wore these in the 1950s.

Leather uppers

Metal spikes tacked to soles

Early caps had very low crowns…

…and very short bills.

Note longer sleeves.

Leather belt

Pants fall to just below knees.

High socks, before stirrups

STAR MODELS
Detroit's Hall of Fame outfielder Ty Cobb (left) and "Shoeless" Joe Jackson of the Chicago White Sox model uniforms worn in the Majors before World War I. Compare the baggy wool pants and jerseys to the sleek, tight-fitting uniforms of today's players. The thick wool of the uniforms made keeping them clean difficult, and they were almost permanently stained with grass and dirt.

WEARIN' O' THE GREEN
Spring training is a time for fun. Each March 17, as clubs play exhibition games in Florida and Arizona, several teams celebrate St. Patrick's Day by donning special green-trimmed uniforms. This one, complete with shamrock on the sleeve, was worn by Hall of Fame pitcher Tom Seaver when he was with the Cincinnati Reds. For one day each spring, the team becomes the Cincinnati Greens.

Batting glove

Batting helmet
with ear flap

White home
jersey

MAYS
24

RETIRED NUMBERS
Teams "retire" jersey numbers to honor their greatest
heroes. No Giants player, for instance, will ever wear
Willie Mays's number 24 again.

Wristbands

Long-sleeved
undershirt

Leather belt

CLASSIC PINSTRIPES
All-Star shortstop Derek Jeter of the
NewYork Yankees models one of
baseball's classic uniforms: the
Yankee pinstripes. These
uniforms, worn at home by the
Bronx Bombers, have barely
changed in color and logo
from the days of Mickey
Mantle and Yogi Berra,
but greatly changed in
style. Like all baseball
uniforms today, they are
body-hugging, stretch
cotton-poly blends made
for comfort, durability, and
protection. Teams also have
a different uniform for road
games, usually in a basic gray
and with their city name
instead of their team name. As
in the old days, a baseball
uniform consists of a jersey,
pants, hat, and socks. Many
players also wear sliding shorts
(above) under their pants. These
shorts have padded thighs that
cushion players' legs and rear when
they slide into bases.

Old-fashioned
high socks

Uniform
pants,
modern
full-length
style

High-topped
baseball
spikes

OLD IS NEW AGAIN
To revive interest in the "old
days," in 1996 Major League
teams wore "throwback"
uniforms in tribute to previous
incarnations of their teams.
Texas Rangers catcher Ivan
Rodriguez ran the bases in the
uniform of a Texas Rangers
minor league team from
the 1950s.

Pitching

Four-seam fastball

Two-seam fastball

Curveball

"Circle" change-up

Knuckleball

THE PITCHER'S MOUND is the center of the baseball universe. Nothing happens in a baseball game until the pitcher starts his windup and fires in that first pitch. His job is to get the opposing hitters out, but saying that and doing it are two very different things. Warren Spahn (363 wins, most by a left-hander) said, "Hitting is the art of timing. Pitching is the art of upsetting timing." A wide variety of types of pitches (left) is used to upset a hitter's timing. An even wider variety of arm motions, leg motions, and body spins has also been put to use over the years. And until the 1930s, pitchers could legally deface a ball, whether by cutting it or applying all sorts of "foreign substances" (including spit) to make it harder to hit. It's a tough job—pitchers need all the help they can get.

RECORD-SETTING CLOSER
Los Angeles Dodgers relief pitcher Eric Gagne has become one of the most feared pitchers in baseball. From 2002 to 2004, he converted an amazing 84 consecutive save opportunities. A "closer" get a save when he comes into the game in a tight situation and finishes off the win for his team. Gagne has a great fastball, but an even more devastating changeup.

GETTING A GRIP
Different pitches are thrown using different grips (above). Pitchers determine how a ball moves or curves by changing the position of their fingers on the raised seams of the ball, or by turning their wrist.

Pitchers focus their eyes on their target: the catcher's mitt.

Pitcher's glove

Pitchers drive toward home by pushing off the pitching rubber with their back foot.

Set position — The stride — Driving off back foot

Hand behind head — Arm whips forward — Follow-through — Ready to field

GOING THROUGH THE MOTION

If hitting, in the words of Mark McGwire, is one of the "hardest things in sports," then pitching is a close second. Pitchers have their own style of "delivery," but whether they throw over the top, from three quarters, or sidearm, they all have one aim—throw the ball past the hitter in the strike zone. All pitchers begin their deliveries from one of two positions: the set position, used with men on base, and the windup, used with the bases empty. The set helps deliver the ball more quickly, reducing the time for runners to attempt steals.

SMOKIN' SOX
In 1999, Boston's Pedro Martinez, the 1997 Cy Young Award winner with Montreal, became only the second pitcher to win the award in each league.

511
Watching many of baseball's legendary records fall in recent years (Roger Maris's 61 homers, Lou Gehrig's 2,130 consecutive games played, Ty Cobb's 4,192 hits), it would be easy to say that any record is breakable. One that most assuredly is not is the career victory total of Denton True "Cy" Young, who earned 511 wins from 1890-1911. He won more than 30 games in a season five times. He combined durability with power and guile to dominate baseball's early years. Today, the annual A.L. and N.L. awards for the best pitcher are named after him.

Flimsy non-webbed glove

BOSTON

Baggy wool uniform

High-topped shoes

FIVE FABULOUS SEASONS
From 1962-66, Sandy Koufax of the Dodgers was the greatest pitcher of all time. The left-hander's sizzling fastball and devastating curve yielded three Cy Young Awards, five ERA titles, and four no-hitters. His 27 wins in 1966 were the most by a lefty in the 1900s. Sadly, arthritis forced him to retire after that season.

Fastball grip

SPEED FROM THE EAST
Hideo Nomo became the first Japanese-born pitcher to throw a no-hitter while with the Dodgers in 1996. A no-hitter is one of the greatest feats a pitcher can perform, holding the opposing team to no hits for an entire game.

IT'S ALL ABOUT SPEED
More so than ever before, pitchers are judged by how fast they can throw the ball. Movement and control are vital, too, but speed rules. Few baseball scouts go anywhere without a radar gun (left) to measure pitch speed. You probably won't reach the Major Leagues unless your fastball reaches 90 miles per hour. Hit 100 and you earn a fast-track ticket to "The Show" (the big leagues).

Catching

Yogi Berra

On tag plays, catchers often remove their masks for better visibility.

THE HARDEST WORKING PLAYER on a baseball team is the catcher. Squatting behind home plate for nine innings, he must catch everything a pitcher throws past a hitter, must endure being hit by foul tips and bats, and must be ready to fire perfect throws to catch would-be base stealers. Occasionally, he must deal with charging runners, who plow into him like a football fullback, or he must soothe a pitcher's shattered ego after a home run. The great Yankee manager Casey Stengel summed up the importance of the catcher when he said, "Ya gotta have a catcher. Otherwise the ball will roll all the way back to the backstop.

PLAY AT THE PLATE!

One of baseball's most exciting plays occurs when ball and runner arrive at home plate at the same time. The catcher must block the plate and make the tag. Here Ivan Rodriguez, baseball's best catcher, does just that. Rodriguez also excels at picking off base runners with a throwing arm called one of the best ever.

JUST LIKE THE PROS

Playing catcher in a youth baseball league is just as grueling as the pros. Like their Major League role models, young catchers wear all the protective gear available, including mask, helmet, chest protector, shin guards, and protective cup. It sometimes takes young players a while to adjust to the gear, but after a few foul tips, they'll find it's worth the effort.

Detachable throat protector

Extra-long youth chest protector

Shin guards with knee cups

CAMPY

After eight seasons in the Negro Leagues, Roy Campanella joined the Brooklyn Dodgers in 1948 and redefined the catching position. Combining power at the plate with great catching skills, "Campy" won three MVP awards in the 1950s. Sadly, a 1958 auto accident left him partially paralyzed. However, he remained close to the game and was one of baseball's most beloved figures until his death in 1993.

Campanella in 1950s Wheaties ad

FROM ICE TO DIAMOND

Most catcher's equipment has changed only in materials rather than form. The iron-barred catcher's mask of today looks much like that used in the 1930s. However, a recent innovation is changing that. Inspired by masks used by hockey goalies, catcher Charlie O'Brien helped design this model, which allows for more protection and greater visibility.

Elastic strap

CATCHING WITH A PILLOW

Early catcher's mitts (right) were little more than round leather pillows with space for the hand to fit into the back. The pocket was developed over time by catching the ball. There was little or no hinge or webbing. Most catchers needed to use both hands to catch. Modern gloves (opposite, top right) have made catching safer by letting catchers use only one hand.

Very small webbing area

Pocket formed at center over time.

Removable sun visor

Chest protector is lower on throwing shoulder to allow better range of motion for throwing.

Catcher's mask with attached throat protector

"THE TOOLS OF IGNORANCE"

Mickey Cochrane (below) coined that phrase to describe the protective gear worn by catchers. And while catching is indeed a tough job most players avoid, today's equipment makes it safer than ever. From head to toe, catchers wear heavy-duty padding or high-impact plastic coverings that shield them from most of the bumps and bruises the position creates. But as any catcher will tell you, foul balls have a way to finding an unprotected spot. Catchers are generally not too tall, and are some of the most powerful baseball players. But they also must be among the most nimble and flexible. They spend most of their time on the field standing up and squatting down repeatedly.

JUST HIT THE MITT

The modern catcher's mitt looks more like other fielder's gloves, with a built-in pocket and wide webbing. Catcher's mitts have more padding on the edges, and are also designed to make it easier to scoop out or backhand low pitches.

FLASHING THE SIGNALS

Catchers use hand signals to tell pitchers what pitch they should throw. Each team develops its own set of signals, but the classic list is one finger for a fastball, two for a curve, three for a change, and four for any other pitch thrown, such as a slider. Signals are changed when runners are on base, so the runners can't tip off the hitters with their own signals. Catchers also can signal for pitchouts or pickoffs.

Fielding glove worn under mitt

The catcher's squat position

CATCHING AND HITTING

Catchers traditionally are depended on for defense. If they can hit, then so much the better. Hall of Fame catcher Mickey Cochrane, here demonstrating a throw to second base, was one of the best hitting catchers, with a lifetime average of .320. Cincinnati's Johnny Bench, another Hall of Famer, was an outstanding hitter as well as top defender. Among today's catchers, the Rangers' Ivan Rodriguez and the Mets' Mike Piazza star at the plate as well as behind it. Piazza especially has shone, with six consecutive .300 seasons. His .362 mark in 1997 was the best by a catcher in the 1900s.

Shin guards hinged around knees

Old-style chest protector

Flaps protect feet

Smaller, old-style leather shin guards

Infield and Outfield

The shortstop is usually the best fielder on a team. He has to be quick, fast, accurate, and smart. Here Alex Cintron of the Diamondbacks demonstrates excellent form for fielding ground balls. Infielders need to stay low and balanced, watch the ball fall into their glove, and make a quick, accurate throw to the base. At the crack of the bat, an infielder moves to intercept the ball, scoop up the grounder in his mitt, and quickly grab the ball with the throwing hand.

ON DEFENSE, A BASEBALL TEAM HAS TWO MAIN PARTS: infield and outfield. The four players who play near the bases form the infield. The three players who play out beyond the bases are the outfield. (The pitcher and catcher are officially part of the infield.) Each of the four infield positions—first base, second base, shortstop, and third base—has a special area of responsibility as well as skills particular to that area. The three outfield spots—left field, center field, and right field—are more similar. Each covers about one-third of the outfield. But no matter what their specialty, all of these players have one job when the ball is put into play: Get the runners out and stop runs from scoring.

THE WIZARD OF OZ
Few players in recent years have been as spectacular in the field as Hall of Fame shortstop Ozzie Smith, who played for the Padres and Cardinals from 1978–96. His range, his ability to dive and come up throwing, and his stunning dives made him into one of the best defensive players ever at the most important defensive position.

Running forward, Mondesi sights his target.

A CANNON IN RIGHT
Right fielders normally have the strongest throwing arm on a team because they have to make the longest throws, from deep in right to third base. Rightfielder Raul Mondesi shows how outfielders charge the ball and use their momentum to help make their throws carry farther. Mondesi won two Gold Gloves, thanks in part to one of the strongest and most accurate arms in the majors.

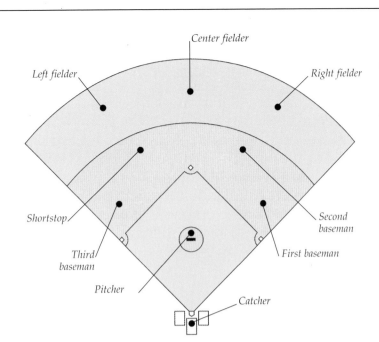

Center fielder

Left fielder

Right fielder

Shortstop

Second baseman

Third baseman

First baseman

Pitcher

Catcher

BASEBALL DEFENSIVE POSITIONS
The diagram above shows the basic position that each player on a baseball team takes prior to each pitch. Players adjust their positions slightly depending on the hitter or the game situation. Some examples—Against a right-handed pull hitter, the shortstop, left fielder, and center fielder may move to their right. With a runner on third and less than two outs, the infield will play "in," or at the edge of the grass nearer to home plate. On a bunt play, the first and third basemen will charge toward the plate to field the bunt and throw to a base.

"HE LEAPS AT THE WALL, AND…"
Some of baseball's most spectacular plays come when an outfielder jumps to reach over the wall to turn a would-be home run into a long out. Here Detroit's Bobby Higginson has raced to the wall in center, timed his jump just right, and stretched out to catch the ball before it reaches the seats.

BARRY IN THE OUTFIELD
San Francisco's Barry Bonds has gained fame for his mighty homers. But he has also won eight Gold Gloves for outfield play. He combines a great throwing arm with speed and outstanding leaping ability. Here Bonds demonstrates an important outfield technique: catching fly balls. Outfielders need to see a fly ball off the bat and react quickly. They first move to where they think it will land, and then put their glove up for the catch. On sunny days, they use their glove to shield their eyes from the sun, and attempt to track the ball in the glare. It's tricky, but with practice, it becomes routine.

Even while jumping, an accurate throw is vital.

TWO FOR ONE
The "pitcher's best friend," a double play happens when two outs are recorded on one batted ball, normally a grounder.
For instance, the ball is hit to the second baseman, who throws it to the shortstop at second base. The shortstop steps on second to force out a runner coming from first (and often leaps to avoid the sliding runner, as shown here by Omar Vizquel), and then throws to first to get the batter.

The left arm balances, while the right arm rears back.

Outfielders put their whole body into their throws.

Mondesi pushes off with back leg.

29

Batting

Stan Musial used his odd batting style to total 3,630 hits, fourth all-time.

MARK MCGWIRE SAID IT FOR ALL PLAYERS: Hitting a baseball is the single most difficult feat in sports. The greatest hitters—or batters, the terms are interchangeable—succeed only about three times out of ten. A basketball player with that success rate would be out of a job; a field-goal kicker wouldn't make the football team. But batting is so hard to do well that .300 is the gold standard. In less than a third of a second, batters must decide to swing, begin their swing, and then, another tiny fraction of a second later, somehow connect a rounded bat with a wildly spinning round ball that is flying toward them at speeds that can reach more than 90 miles per hour. It is hard to do, but when it is done well, wow…what a singularly thrilling moment.

Ready to hit

Shoulder turn begins

Eyes on the ball

Wrists turn over

Full follow-through

IT SURE _LOOKS_ EASY
This sequence of photos shows proper, classic hitting form. However, each player adapts this basic form to his or her needs and particular abilities. Some players will begin the swing with the bat higher or lower, or will take a short or long step with their front foot. The keys to a successful swing, though, are the same no matter what style a batter uses: consistency, keeping the eyes on the ball, and remaining smooth and quick throughout. Put all these things together, swing at the right pitch, and a hit is often the result.

Cobb played in the days before batting helmets.

Junior joined Cincinnati in 2002; his dad had starred for the Reds in the 1970s.

OH, WHAT A HITTER
The major leagues are not the only place to find great hitters. Sadaharu Oh of the Tokyo Giants used his unusual batting style—lifting his right leg as he strode into the pitch—to hit an international record 868 career home runs in more than 3,000 fewer at-bats than major league career leader Hank Aaron.

Bat cocked toward pitcher

Gwynn demonstrates "hitting off the front foot."

THE GEORGIA PEACH
Hall of Fame outfielder Ty Cobb held his hands several inches apart on the bat, a style that no one successfully imitated. No one could match his talent, either. Cobb (Detroit, 1905-1928) used that odd style to compile a major-league record .366 lifetime average and 4,192 hits, second-most all-time.

JUNIOR
A long, looping, uppercut swing would spell disaster for most hitters. For Cincinnati centerfielder Ken Griffey, Jr., that stroke has spelled power. "Junior" reached 350 career home runs faster than any player in major-league history.

High kick with front leg

Eyes on the ball

Firm, but
not tight,
grip

While Gwynn has
powerful legs, his
hands are the key to
his success.

"THE GREATEST HITTER WHO EVER LIVED"

This sequence (clockwise from top left) shows the form of Ted Williams, the Red Sox outfielder whose childhood dream was to be the greatest hitter of all time. His dream came true. Williams posted a lifetime average of .344 with 521 home runs, even though he gave up five seasons to military service. Combining power, average, and an unerring eye, the "Splendid Splinter" could flat-out hit.

THE BEST IN THE GAME...TODAY

San Diego's sweet-swinging outfielder Tony Gwynn is the only active player in the all-time top 20 in career batting average. He is an eight-time National League batting champion, had more than 200 hits in five different seasons, and has hit over .300 every year since 1983. Gwynn has nearly perfect form at the plate, and his quick wrists allow him to be as adept at pulling the ball as he is "going the other way," that is, hitting an outside pitch to left field, which is the other way for a lefty. In 1998, he became the 21st player to reach 3,000 hits in his career.

Youth
league
face mask

Fingers
cradle bat
lightly to
let bat "give"
with the
pitch.

Hips and
shoulders square
to face pitcher.

Ventilated for
comfort

FIT LIKE A GLOVE

While old-timers such as Cobb and Williams would have no use for them, batting gloves are essential for all but a handful of today's players. The leather and nylon gloves give players surer grip on the bat.

TRI-CURVE

Franklin

Velcro wrist
closures

LAY ONE DOWN, KID

A special type of hit is called the "bunt." The batter pushes the pitch softly so that it stays between the pitcher's mound and home plate. The batter usually is put out on a "sacrifice" bunt, but the runners on base advance.

Baserunning

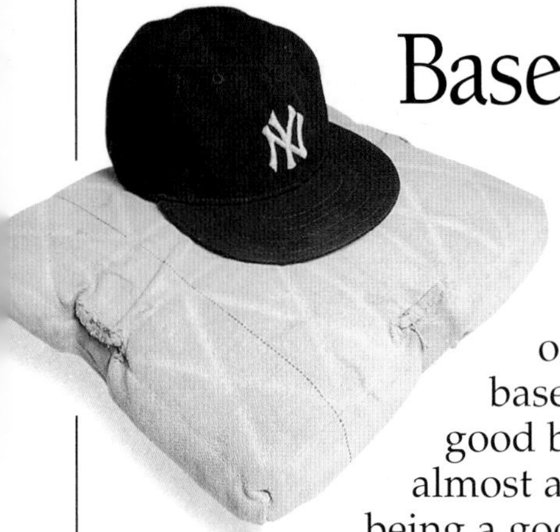

O<small>NCE A BATTER</small>
REACHES BASE
(1950s bag, left), he
or she becomes a
base runner. Being a
good base runner is
almost as important as
being a good hitter. If you
can't make your way around the bases to
score, it doesn't matter how often you get on
base. Base runners advance from base to
base when their teammates put the ball in
play. They also can advance by stealing a
base or on a passed ball or wild pitch,
which is when a pitch gets by the catcher.
Every base runner has one ultimate goal:
Step on home plate and score a run for the
team. A base runner must always be alert
to the situation—how many outs are there?
What's the count? Who is pitching? Where
are the fielders? These variables change on
every pitch, so concentration is as vital to a
base runner as speed and technique.

Home plate umpire in position to make the call

SPEED DEMON
Speedy Dave Roberts demonstrates
how a runner begins to steal a base;
that is, running as the pitch is thrown
to the plate and reaching the next base
safely. Steals are a huge
offensive advantage for
a team. A stolen base
disrupts a pitcher's
timing and sets up
runners to score.

A good jump is key for a base stealer.

HE'S OUT!
One of the hardest things for young players to
learn is one of baseball's most unique skills:
sliding. When running hard toward a base,
sliding on the dirt is the only way to safely
stop momentum and keep from going
past the base. A safe slide (shown
here) has the head up, the top leg
pointed toward the base, and
the bottom leg tucked
underneath.

Runner diving back to first

Fielder in good position to make tag

Players slide on their thighs.

Batting glove

Until Jackie Robinson joined the Brooklyn Dodgers in 1947, no black man had played Major League baseball. For decades, racism kept thousands of great athletes out of the game until the courageous Robinson broke the barrier. With incredible inner strength to face down outright bigotry, and fantastic baseball skills, most notably his speed and daring on the base paths, Robinson led the way.

Robinson stole home 19 times in his career.

Books about Robinson from the 1940s and 1950s

PICKOFF PLAY

These young players are demonstrating a pickoff play at first base. One way that pitchers keep potential base stealers from getting too big a lead is to throw to first instead of to home. A good pickoff move can sometimes catch a runner napping, and the first baseman can make the tag for the out.

THE BEST KIND OF RUNNING

Devon White of the Los Angeles Dodgers demonstrates every player's favorite kind of baserunning: the home run trot. When the ball leaves the park, players enjoy a more leisurely trip around the bases. Only a real show-off does anything other than a simple jog.

Base anchored to ground

Hands reach for base.

Back foot on base

THE MAN OF STEALS

Rickey Henderson is shown here demonstrating a headfirst slide (the technique is also shown by Kerry Robinson on the cover; note how he reaches for the bag with his fingers up to avoid jamming them). Henderson is baseball's all-time leader in stolen bases, with a career total of more than 1,400 (more than 500 more than Lou Brock in second place). Henderson led the American League in steals 12 times, and in 1982 he set the single-season record with 130 while with Oakland. Henderson's skills made him into the greatest leadoff hitter in baseball history.

Hey, Blue!

Baseball is a game of rules, and the people charged with enforcing those rules are called umpires. Umpires determine, or "call," whether a pitch is a ball or a strike…they call base runners safe or out…they decide whether a batted ball is foul or fair. In the Major Leagues, four umpires are used in regular-season games, six in the playoffs and World Series. One of the four "umps" works behind home plate, while the others are stationed at each of the three bases. At lower levels of baseball, anywhere from one to four umpires are used. Umpires have a tough job. Baseball is a fast-moving game, so umps must make split-second decisions that can mean victory or defeat for one team or the other. Why "Hey, blue"? Although baseball umpires appear to be wearing black, their uniforms usually are dark navy blue. So no matter what his name is, any baseball umpire will respond to the name "Blue."

OLD-TIME GEAR
Until the 1970s, home plate umpires wore a large chest protector outside their coat. This model from the 1930s was heavy leather, bulky, and hard to manage. Today's umpires wear thinner, lighter gear under their uniform shirts.

THE BRUSH OFF
Umpires need a clean, clear view of home plate. The home plate umpire carries a small brush (an older model is pictured) to wipe off the plate periodically. Umpires always turn their back to the field before bending down and dusting.

Thumb wheel

STRIKE BALL

OUT

INNING

KEEPING TRACK
All umpires carry handheld "indicators" (older model, left; newer version, right) that help them keep track of the number of outs, balls, strikes and innings. While fans look to scoreboards for this information, the umpires have the final say.

THE RHUBARB
Every judgement call by an umpire upsets at least one of the two teams in the game. When a team's manager is especially upset, he comes on to the field to argue with the umpire. This can be a simple discussion, as here with the Yankees' manager Joe Torre, or a hat-flinging, dust-kicking, nose-to-nose screaming match. Managers and players are ejected automatically for arguing about balls and strikes.

Umpires have uniform numbers, too.

Many managers wear sneakers, not baseball spikes.

Indication of ejection

Dark blue shirt

Gray pants

YOU'RE OUTTA HERE!
When an umpire feels a player or manager has argued too much or has stepped beyond the bounds of sportsmanship, the umpire ejects that manager or player from the game. The ejected person must leave the dugout and return to the clubhouse. The leagues may also impose fines or additional suspensions for particularly bad sportsmanship.

Signal for a strike

Sun visor

Shoulder pads protect ump from foul tips.

Face mask

Chest protector is under shirt.

Ball bag

Steel-toed shoes

BEHIND THE PLATE

The home plate umpire has the toughest job on the umpiring crew. He must make split-second decisions on whether a pitch is a ball or strike, must judge any bunts fair or foul, and must make calls on close plays at the plate. Each home plate umpire develops his own personal style for calling strikes. Some are subtle, some are loud and dramatic. Also, like a catcher, the home plate umpire wears protective gear, including a chest protector, face mask, shin guards, and heavy shoes.

HE'S IN THERE!

This umpire shows he has called the runner "safe" by spreading his arms wide. Early pro umpires did not use hand signals. When a deaf pro player named "Dummy" Hoy couldn't hear heir vocal calls, a system of signals was developed to help him. It then caught on and is still used today.

HE'S OUT!

Like home plate umpires with their personal strike calls, base umpires develop their own unique ways of calling a player "out." This umpire from college baseball demonstrates the classic "punch-out" style after the fielder has applied the tag to the runner. Other umps use an outstretched thumb on one hand or form an "L" with their arm held away from their body.

FAIR OR FOUL?

Umpires at first and third base determine if batted balls are fair or foul. This umpire is indicating a fair ball by pointing toward fair territory. The ball must hit the ground within the white line to be a fair ball.

Cards and Stats

BASEBALL WITHOUT STATISTICS would be like chocolate milk without chocolate. The thousands of numbers that swirl around baseball like confetti are the lifeblood of the game. Stats allow fans to compare players of today and yesterday; to marvel at 500 home runs or 300 wins; to argue whether Roger Clemens could out-pitch Walter Johnson; to support a claim that Jackie Robinson was better than Joe Morgan. Baseball has stats for everything from pitching to hitting to baserunning. You might not ever need to know how well a player hits left-handers in night road games in June with less than two outs, but in baseball, you can find that out if you really want to. One of the ways that fans have enjoyed seeing all these stats is on baseball cards. These little rectangles of cardboard have helped fans keep track of their heroes since the pro game began in the 1870s. While every sport has cards now, baseball had them first.

EARLY CARDBOARD HEROES
The card on the left features ace pitcher Mordecai "Three-Finger" Brown (1903-16), who finished his career with a 2.06 career ERA, third-lowest all-time. (A childhood accident cost him parts of two fingers). On the right is Michael "King" Kelly, who was, until Babe Ruth came along, the most famous baseball player in America. He played for four National League teams from 1878-93, earned the highest salary of the day, and had a famous song composed in his honor—"Slide, Kelly, Slide."

NO SMOKING
This piece of cardboard is worth more than $600,000. Only a handful of this 1910 Honus Wagner card exists, and its rarity plus the baseball collecting craze has helped drive its value up. This card, sold with packs of tobacco, is rare because Wagner objected to smoking, and asked that his image not be used. The few cards that did make it onto the market have become the most valuable in the sports card world.

AN AMERICAN HERO
In 1947, Jackie Robinson not only became the first African-American player in Major League history, he became the first black player with a baseball card. He became an instant hero to black fans everywhere, and this card was one way that his fans could carry their hero with them. In later years, as the importance of his career became more apparent, Robinson memorabilia became popular among collectors. New items were produced in 1997 for the fiftieth anniversary of his historic first season.

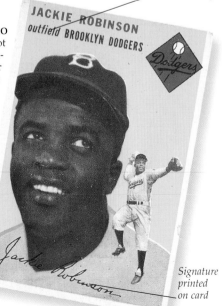

Robinson actually played first and second base, not outfield.

Signature printed on card

GETTING FANCY
As printing technologies have evolved, card designs have gotten wilder. Today's cards often include embossing, gold leaf lettering, holograms, day-glo inks, or sparkling paper. This Topps card of Kirby Puckett, who was one of baseball's most popular players until an eye ailment forced him to retire in 1995, shows another modern trend: special sets. This All-Star set joins rookie sets, award-winner sets, superstar sets, and many others that helped fuel a boom in card collecting. Dozens of companies produce millions of cards each year, making the chances of finding a rare one pretty rare indeed.

Shown in pregame warm-up gear

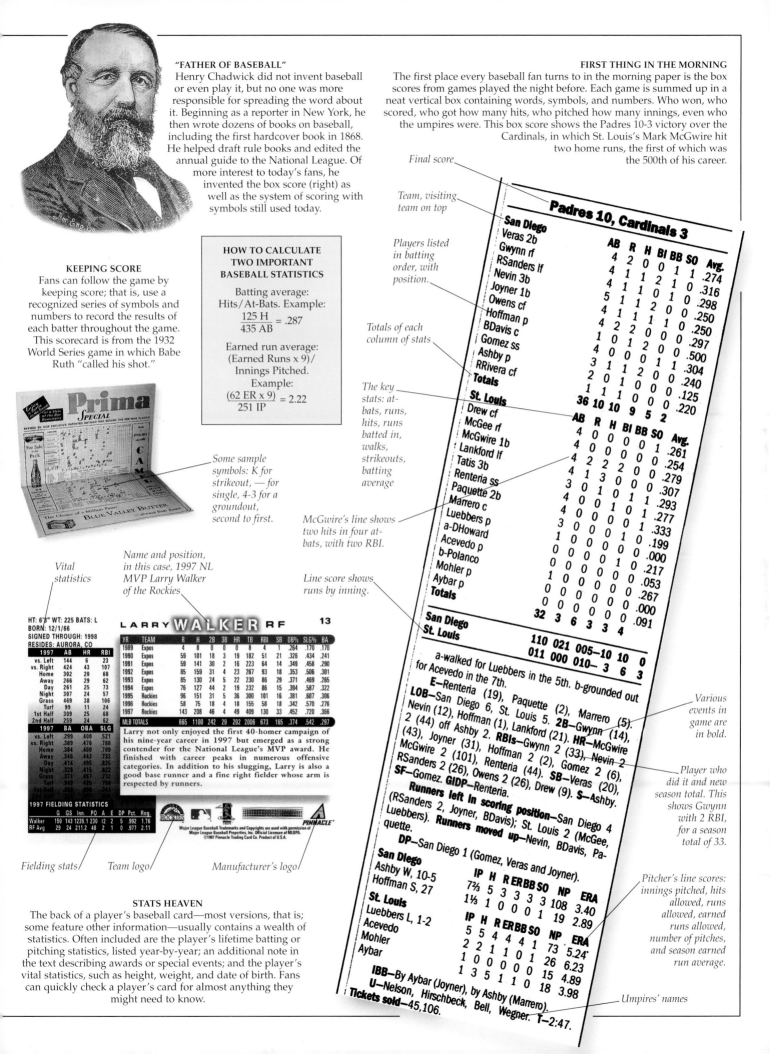

"FATHER OF BASEBALL"

Henry Chadwick did not invent baseball or even play it, but no one was more responsible for spreading the word about it. Beginning as a reporter in New York, he then wrote dozens of books on baseball, including the first hardcover book in 1868. He helped draft rule books and edited the annual guide to the National League. Of more interest to today's fans, he invented the box score (right) as well as the system of scoring with symbols still used today.

KEEPING SCORE

Fans can follow the game by keeping score; that is, use a recognized series of symbols and numbers to record the results of each batter throughout the game. This scorecard is from the 1932 World Series game in which Babe Ruth "called his shot."

HOW TO CALCULATE TWO IMPORTANT BASEBALL STATISTICS

Batting average:
Hits/At-Bats. Example:
$$\frac{125\ H}{435\ AB} = .287$$

Earned run average:
(Earned Runs x 9)/
Innings Pitched.
Example:
$$\frac{(62\ ER \times 9)}{251\ IP} = 2.22$$

Some sample symbols: K for strikeout, — for single, 4-3 for a groundout, second to first.

Vital statistics

Name and position, in this case, 1997 NL MVP Larry Walker of the Rockies.

HT: 6'3" WT: 225 BATS: L
BORN: 12/1/66
SIGNED THROUGH: 1998
RESIDES: AURORA, CO

Larry not only enjoyed the first 40-homer campaign of his nine-year career in 1997 but emerged as a strong contender for the National League's MVP award. He finished with career peaks in numerous offensive categories. In addition to his slugging, Larry is also a good base runner and a fine right fielder whose arm is respected by runners.

Fielding stats

Team logo

Manufacturer's logo

Major League Baseball Trademarks and Copyrights are used with permission of Major League Baseball Properties, Inc. Official Licensee of MLBPA. ©1997 Pinnacle Trading Card Co. Product of U.S.A.

STATS HEAVEN

The back of a player's baseball card—most versions, that is; some feature other information—usually contains a wealth of statistics. Often included are the player's lifetime batting or pitching statistics, listed year-by-year; an additional note in the text describing awards or special events; and the player's vital statistics, such as height, weight, and date of birth. Fans can quickly check a player's card for almost anything they might need to know.

FIRST THING IN THE MORNING

The first place every baseball fan turns to in the morning paper is the box scores from games played the night before. Each game is summed up in a neat vertical box containing words, symbols, and numbers. Who won, who scored, who got how many hits, who pitched how many innings, even who the umpires were. This box score shows the Padres 10-3 victory over the Cardinals, in which St. Louis's Mark McGwire hit two home runs, the first of which was the 500th of his career.

Final score

Team, visiting team on top

Players listed in batting order, with position.

Totals of each column of stats

The key stats: at-bats, runs, hits, runs batted in, walks, strikeouts, batting average

McGwire's line shows two hits in four at-bats, with two RBI.

Line score shows runs by inning.

Various events in game are in bold.

Player who did it and new season total. This shows Gwynn with 2 RBI, for a season total of 33.

Pitcher's line scores: innings pitched, hits allowed, runs allowed, earned runs allowed, number of pitches, and season earned run average.

Umpires' names

International Baseball

BASEBALL STARTED IN THE U.S., but the game's influence has spread worldwide. Today, more than 100 countries are part of the International Baseball Federation. Baseball has become so popular that it became a full medal sport in the Olympics in 1992. As soon as Americans began playing baseball in the late 1800s, they began to take the game with them as they traveled the world. In 1888, Albert Spalding organized a world tour of baseball teams that visited European, Asian, and African countries. Cuba caught the bug early and became one of the world's baseball hotbeds; its players helped spread the game to other Central and South American countries. American missionaries took the game to Japan in the 1880s, and organized teams have played there ever since. Japan also is home to the largest pro league outside the U.S. There are professional leagues in Italy and Australia, too, among other places. Baseball may be America's National Pastime, but it is fast becoming in international pastime as well.

O CANADA!
Canadian players have long been a part of America's National Pastime. Current Canadian-born stars include former National League MVP Larry Walker of Colorado. Canada is home to two Major League teams: the Toronto Blue Jays and the Montreal Expos. And Canada's amateur teams perform well in events like the Pan Am games (left).

EL BEISBOL
Teams from Cuba perennially triumph at international competitions, and their players are some of the best in the world. Their stars, however, are barred by their government from playing elsewhere professionally. This has not stopped a few from escaping from Cuba to find fame and fortune in America.

BASEBALL IN THE OLYMPICS
When Alexander Cartwright and the Kinckerbocker Base Ball Club were helping develop baseball in the mid-1800s, they probably could not have imagined that more than 100 years later, an Australian player (green helmet below) would execute a perfect take-out slide that a shortstop from the Netherlands (blue uniform) would nimbly avoid as cleanly as any young American player. A sure sign of baseball's international growth is its place in the Olympics. It was a demonstration sport in several Olympics, including 1984 and 1988, and became a full medal sport in 1992, with Cuba winning the first of its two consecutive gold medals.

Cuba's star third baseman Omar Linares

1996 Olympic gold medal

Names in English

Traditional baseball uniform

JAPAN'S YANKEES

Like the New York Yankees in America's Major Leagues, the Tokyo Giants have dominated Japanese baseball. The Giants, who play their games at the palatial Tokyo Dome, are far and away the most popular team; they're also the most successful, having won 29 championships in the past 50 years, including a record nine in a row from 1965-73. All-time home run champion Sadaharu Oh starred for the Giants.

Yoshinobu Takahaski slugs a grand slam in the 1999 opener.

HOPE THEY'RE ALL GOOD CATCHERS

After winning their third Japan Series championship in five years in 1997, Yakult Swallows players gave their manager, Katsuya Nomura, a celebratory toss. Japan has 12 pro teams in the Central and Pacific Leagues that play a 130-game schedule in the spring and summer. Baseball has been played in Japan since the late 1800s.

Uniform uses Mexican national colors of red and green.

VIVA MEXICO!

Mexico has almost as long a tradition of pro baseball as America does. Since the 1930s, American pros have spent the winter in Mexico, improving their game against top competitors. A thriving pro league continues today, with national all-star teams (left) performing well at international tournaments. In addition, many Mexican-born players star in the Major Leagues, including Colorado Rockies third baseman Vinny Castilla.

Cuban player Orestes Kindelan

Flowers and laurels given to winners

COUNTRY TO COUNTRY

The United States and Cuba maintain a decades-long diplomatic separation. But in the summer of 1999, the two countries got together on the baseball field. For the first time, a Major League team, the Baltimore Orioles, traveled to Havana to play the Cuban national team. In return, the Cubans played at Baltimore's Camden Yards. Before the first game, Orioles star Carl Ripkin, Jr., and Cuban superstar Omar Linares enjoyed a little player-to-player international relations.

The Negro Leagues

FROM ITS EARLIEST DAYS, PRO BASEBALL BARRED AFRICAN-AMERICANS FROM TAKING PART. While such behavior would be scorned, not to mention illegal, today, the racist attitudes of the times allowed this discrimination to go on. But while black players could not play in the Major Leagues, nothing was going to stop them from playing the game. As early as the 1870s, all-black amateur teams were competing in the Northeast. By the turn of the century, black pro teams began to be formed, and leagues followed soon after. The "Negro Leagues," as they were known, included some of the greatest players of the century—players whose skills, most observers felt, would have made them Major League legends. The heyday of the Negro Leagues came in the 1930s and 1940s, when a dozen or so teams (including the Birmingham Black Barons, hat upper left) played to packed houses in major cities in the Northeast and Midwest. In 1947, when Jackie Robinson finally became the first black player this century to play in the majors, the Negro Leagues slowly died out. Black players joined Major and minor league teams and took their rightful place as part of the American game.

THE "BLACK BABE RUTH"

Of all the many outstanding players from the Negro Leagues, catcher Josh Gibson was perhaps the greatest player, and a batter of enormous strength. Unofficial records give him more than 900 home runs for his career. In 1931, he was credited with 75 home runs, while his career batting average was above .350. Major Leaguers of the time, including the great pitcher Walter Johnson, recognized Gibson's talents, but knew that he could never show them off on the big stage. In 1972, he became the second Negro League player elected to the Hall of Fame.

Before helmets, catchers wore their hats backward.

Gibson-autographed baseball

THE 42-YEAR-OLD ROOKIE

Leroy "Satchel" Paige was by far the most famous and successful player from the Negro Leagues. While his outstanding control as a pitcher first got him noticed, it was his infectious, cocky, and enthusiastic personality that made him a star. Paige once walked to bases loaded on purpose to face Josh Gibson. Then he struck the great catcher out. On tours of towns across America, Paige would have his fielders sit down behind him, and then routinely strike out the side. In 1948 at the age of 42, he joined the Cleveland Indians and attracted record crowds at every game he pitched.

Book published after Paige joined the Indians.

SATCHEL PAIGE'S own story

Pitchin Man

TWENTY FIVE CENTS

As told to HAL LEBOVITZ

THE FASTEST MAN IN SPIKES

Satchel Paige, a teammate of James "Cool Papa" Bell, claimed that Bell was so fast "he could switch off the light and be in bed before the room got dark." Bell used his blinding speed and great batting stroke to star in the Negro Leagues from 1922-46. He joined the Hall of Fame in 1991.

Paige was elected to the Baseball Hall of Fame in 1971.

Bell played for the Monarchs, Grays, Crawfords, and five other Negro League teams.

Baggy wool pants

TOP TEAMS

Along with the Homestead Grays, who won a record nine consecutive league pennants from 1937-45, the Pittsburgh Crawfords (below) were among the Negro Leagues' greatest teams. Three of the four players pictured here—Oscar Charleston and Josh Gibson on the left and Judy Johnson on the right—are in the Baseball Hall of Fame. Charleston in particular combined speed, defense, and hitting at the highest level of skill. New York Giants manager John McGraw called him the best player in the game, black or white.

A Kid's Game

At LEAST ONCE EVERY SEASON, you hear a major leaguer say, "I sometimes can't believe it. I'm getting paid to play a kid's game." Although baseball didn't start with kids, kids are at the base of the game's support. Millions of boys and girls around the world play baseball, either in organized leagues with teams and uniforms, or with their friends in the backyard, park, or street. Players at the highest levels are doing the same things they did when they were kids: hitting, pitching, and catching. Kids also are tremendous fans of baseball. Visit any Major League park and you'll see hundreds of kids cheering on their heroes or crowding around them afterward for autographs. Baseball may be a game for everyone, but down deep, it is a game for kids.

LITTLE KIDS... BIG-TIME ACTION
Kids play baseball with as much heart and excitement as their Major League heroes. This play at the plate from the 1999 Little League World Series (won by Japan) looks as if it could have come from a big-league game. Both the catcher and the player sliding are showing great form.

MY HERO
Yankees second baseman Chuck Knoblauch (11) seems to be telling this young player, "Someday, maybe you, too, can play at Yankee Stadium." These members of the American runners-up (10) and Japanese champions of the 1999 Little League World Series were honored on the field before a Yankees game.

Team logo

Baseball cap

Aluminum bat

Batting tee

JUST LIKE THE PROS
Baseball at most youth levels is very similar to that played in the Major Leagues. This pitcher from a Santa Barbara, California, Pony League team shows the same form that he sees the big leaguers use on TV. This transfer of the game from old to young helps maintain baseball's popularity.

Baseball pants

TEE IT UP
Many kids get their start in baseball by playing tee ball. Instead of trying to hit a pitched ball, batters take their cuts at a ball placed on a batting tee. After the ball is hit, play continues as in a normal game, with baserunning and defense. Learning a proper batting stroke without worrying how fast the ball is coming in helps train young players so that they're more ready to face live pitching as they get older. Tee ball is popular with both boys and girls, ages 4-8.

Aluminum bat approved for Little League play.

Chin strap

WORLD CHAMPS!
Winning pitcher Kazuki Sumiyama (center) of Japan is greeted by his joyous teammates after he led his team from Osaka to the 1999 Little League World Series championship. Japan defeated a team from Phoenix City, Alabama. Three other teams from the U.S. joined teams from three other international regions in the annual Series. Sumiyama's countryman Tatsuya Sugata (left) helped Japan finish second in the 1998 series.

Batting helmet with ear flaps

Logo of international area represented

Leather belt

GIRLS, TOO? YOU BET!
Thousands of girls take part in youth baseball leagues at all levels. Girls have appeared in the Little League World Series and have played on high school teams. A few girls have played in college, too. Girls can be just as good as boys at hitting, pitching, fielding, and baserunning. Traditionally, only boys played baseball...but that has certainly changed today.

Traditional baseball pants with stirrup socks

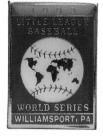

CHAMPS FROM THE FAR EAST
The Little League World Series has been held every summer since 1954. In the beginning, only U.S. teams took part. Mexico was the first international team to win the Series in 1957. Four U.S. teams reached the finals, along with teams from the Far East, Europe, Canada, and Central/South America. In 2000, the tournament field expands to 16 teams. The teams are all-star teams and all the players must come from one league. Teams from Taiwan have had the most success among international teams, winning 16 Series. Japan won the Series in 1999.

A BASEBALL TRADITION
The Little League World Series is wonderful fun for the players and coaches, as well as a great show of baseball talent for the fans. It's also a place to enjoy the popular hobby of collecting and trading souvenir pins (above). Pin traders gather different pins from teams and leagues around the world for their collections.

Women in Baseball

Some players wear visors instead of caps.

No woman has ever played in a major league game. But that has not stopped millions of women and girls from taking part in baseball. From little girls starting out in tee ball to a handful of professional women's baseball teams, there are many opportunities for girls to play the game. One of the most popular ways is softball, a form of baseball played on a smaller diamond with a bigger ball. Women and girls usually play fast-pitch softball, in which the ball is thrown underhand as fast as boys throw overhand. In the United States, there are women's pro softball leagues, and many foreign countries send women's teams to play Olympic softball. Young girls also play in organized baseball leagues, including Little League and Pony League. Since 1988, several girls have even appeared in the Little League World Series. Women work too as umpires and coaches in youth leagues.

DAISIES — Fort Wayne — Major League GIRLS BASEBALL — 1953 OFFICIAL PROGRAM and SCORE BOOK 15¢

Softball shorts

Softball gloves are usually larger than baseball gloves.

NOT BAD... FOR A GIRL

In 1931, Jackie Mitchell (above) signed a pro contract with the minor league Chattanooga Lookouts. In an exhibition, she struck out Lou Gehrig and Babe Ruth (standing), but no one knows for sure how hard they tried. In any case, Mitchell never got her chance in a real game. The baseball commissioner voided her contract on the grounds that the game was "too strenuous for women."

SOFTBALL SUPERSTARS

Fast-pitch softball is one way that many girls and women take part in a sport much like baseball. Pitchers, such as Lisa Fernandez, who led the U.S. to the 1996 Olympic gold medal, throw underhand at speeds reaching 80 miles per hour. The bases are only 60 feet apart, as opposed to 90. The ball is about 40 percent bigger than a baseball, but is not, as the name of the sport implies, soft. Beyond that, softball at this level and baseball are much the same, with outs, strikes, balls, innings, and runs. Pitching is more dominant in softball, however, since the mound is only 45 feet from home plate; thus, scores are usually lower. Although young girls may play youth baseball, most play in organized softball leagues. High schools and colleges have fast-pitch softball programs, too.

First baseman's glove

Long-sleeved shirt

AAGBL players wore skirts.

Knee socks

STARS OF THE SILVER SCREEN
Interest in the AAGBL grew in the 1980s when former players began lobbying to have more of the history of the league included in the Hall of Fame. Their campaign helped push development of the movie A League of Their Own, which featured the Rockford Peaches.

Same type of glove as male players

A LEAGUE OF THEIR OWN
In 1943, with the Major Leagues depleted due to World War II, Chicago Cubs owner Philip Wrigley started a professional women's softball league to drum up fan interest. The All-American Girls Baseball League (AAGBL) began play that year in South Bend, Indiana; Racine, Wisconsin; Rockford, Illinois; and Kenosha, Wisconsin. Nearly 200,000 fans came out to watch the games, and attendance increased a few years later when the league switched from playing softball and pitching underhand to playing baseball.

MORE TEAMS COME TO PLAY
The growth of the AAGBL continued after World War II. The Peoria Redwings joined the AAGBL in 1946 and played each season until 1951. The small midwestern city of Peoria was typical of the hometowns of the teams. The teams relied on support form small communities and avoided big-league competition.

PEORIA ILL.

BORDERS CRACKS THE BARRIER
In 1994, left-handed pitcher Ila Borders, the MVP of her high school team, because the first woman to win a college game. She played three years at Southern California College and one at Whittier College. In 1997, the publicity-minded St. Paul Saints of the independent Northern League signed Borders to a pro contract, where she became the first woman to start and win a professional baseball game. Borders also later played for the Duluth-Superior Dukes. Her success helped spur the short-lived Ladies Baseball League in 1997 and the traveling Colorado Spring Bullets team in 1997-98. Women still do not have a major place in professional baseball, but it's not for lack of trying.

Jerseys styled after women's blouses

ANYTHING FOR PUBLICITY
By 1948, the AAGBL had 10 teams in Midwestern towns and cities; nearly one million fans attended games during the 1948 season. Former Major League stars such as Jimmie Foxx and Max Carey were hired to manage the teams. And while much of the publicity surrounding the league focused on the players as women, they also gained respect for their skills on the diamond. Unfortunately, with Major Leaguers returning from the war, interest in the women's league began to die out. The AAGBL played its last season in 1954.

Team logo on cap

All the managers were male.

Stirrup socks

Shoes similar to baseball spikes

Ballparks

POETS HAVE WRITTEN about ballparks. Songs are composed in honor of parks. The brilliant green grass, the contrasting brown infield, the shirt-sleeved crowd, the pastoral nature of the ball yard—all evoke feelings one doesn't get from a basketball arena or gigantic football stadium. The thrill baseball fans get from that first glimpse of green as they walk through a tunnel toward their seats is unlike any other in sports. Fathers and mothers and sons and daughters today take that walk together, just as parents and children have for decades. Even today, as new parks spring up all over, they often are designed to feel like old ballparks. With the sense of history that baseball creates, a ballpark is more than just a place where two teams play; it is, as the movie said, a field of dreams.

Christy Mathewson

FAN FOR FANS
Whether a hand-held fan honoring a baseball hero or a pin made for Mother's Day (far left), there have been promotional items created for ballpark fans from baseball's earliest days. Special days are held throughout the season at which fans get everything from bats to beach towels to Beanie Babies. ™

Usher's cap and ID pin

THE SEAT WHERE THEY LIVED
This is a bleacher seat from Crosley Field, home of the Cincinatti Reds from 1912-70. The fabled old field was demolished in 1970 and the Reds moved to the more modern, but less charming Riverfront Stadium, now known as Cinergy Field.

Outfield bleachers

HOME OF "DA BUMS"
Few cities have ever had a closer relationship to a ballpark than did Brooklyn, New York, to Ebbets Field. The tiny bandbox of a stadium was home to the Dodgers from 1913 to 1957, when the team broke millions of local hearts and moved to Los Angeles. On the right field fence, clothier Abe Stark Posted a billboard that read, "Hit this sign, win free suit."

Upper deck

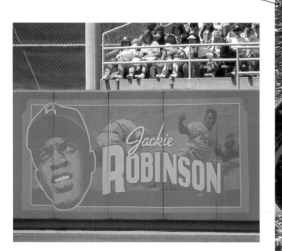

HONORING JACKIE
In 1997, on the fiftieth anniversary of Jackie Robinson becoming the first African-American in the modern major leagues, Major League Baseball announced that Robinson's number 42 would be retired by every club. Each team now honors Robinson somewhere in its stadium, such as this mural in Dodger Stadium.

FRIENDLY CONFINES
One of baseball's most revered ballparks is Wrigley Field, home of the Chicago Cubs. Ivy (right) grows on its brick outfield walls. Fans can watch from the roofs of apartment buildings located behind the stadium.

Distance in feet from home plate

ULTRA-MODERN
The Skydome, home of the Toronto Blue Jays, was the first sports stadium with a retractable roof. The large, curved portion at the top slides along tracks to cover the field and the fans in case of bad weather. Seattle's Safeco Field and Tampa's Tropicana Field also boast similar technological marvels. Skydome has a hotel and several restaurants inside it, too.

A COZY LITTLE PARK
This aerial view of Tiger Stadium in Detroit shows how the park was squeezed into the neighborhood. That was how the first ballparks were constructed. Compare the cramped feeling of this old ball yard, built in 1912, with the expansive design of Dodger Stadium (below). The Tigers played their last game on this field in 1999, moving to Comerica Park for the 2000 season. Some fans bemoan the loss of these old ballparks (Boston's Fenway Park is now the oldest park in the majors. It, too, opened in 1912). And while most people now agree that vast, impersonal stadiums are not the answer, fans have come out in droves to new stadiums in Baltimore, Cleveland, Arlington, and elsewhere. Why? Because they combine the best features of the old-time parks with modern amenities.

Light tower

Scoreboard

PROGRAMS! GET YOUR PROGRAMS!
Few fans leave a ballpark empty-handed. Concession stands, such as this one at Baltimore's Camden Yards, are located throughout the stadium and offer everything a fan could want.

Box seats

TAKE US OUT TO THE BALLPARK
This panoramic view of Dodger Stadium in Los Angeles shows how most baseball stadiums are laid out. A horseshoe of seats surrounds the field, with the bottom of the U-shape at home plate. Raised bleachers rise up beyond the outfield wall. Most fans think the best seats are behind home plate or along the baselines between the bases and home plate. But some fans swear by the cozy bleachers.

Baseball Hall of Fame

VISITING THE BASEBALL HALL OF FAME IS LIKE TAKING A WALK THROUGH A HISTORY BOOK. Located in Cooperstown, New York, the Hall of Fame contains all of the important artifacts and memorabilia from baseball's past—with more items added every year. On display at the Hall are bats used by Nap Lajoie, Babe Ruth, and Mark McGwire; balls hit by Lou Gehrig, Hank Aaron, and Sammy Sosa; caps worn by Christy Mathewson, Satchel Paige, and Roger Clemens; bases stolen by Ty Cobb, Lou Brock, and Rickey Henderson. There are also thousands of programs, scorecards, posters, pennants, and souvenirs to look at. The Hall's library contains millions of photographs and important baseball records, and serves as a key resource for scholars researching the sport. The most important function of the Hall of Fame, however, is to honor the greatest players, coaches, and contributors in the game. Each year, another class of baseball greats is inducted into the Hall, to remain forever a vital part of baseball's ongoing story.

THE RYAN EXPRESS
Nolan Ryan pitched in the Major Leagues for 27 seasons, the most of any player. His overpowering fastball made him dominant for many of those years. He is the all-time career leader in strikeouts, and set the single-season record in 1973 with 383. Ryan also threw seven no-hitters, the most by any pitcher. The ball above is now on display at the Hall of Fame, where Ryan was inducted in 1999.

GEORGE HOWARD BRETT
KANSAS CITY, A.L., 1973 – 1993

PLAYED EACH GAME WITH CEASELESS INTENSITY AND UNBRIDLED PASSION. LIFETIME MARKS INCLUDE .305 BA, 317 HR, 1,595 RBI AND 3,154 HITS. ELEVEN .300 SEASONS. A 13-TIME ALL-STAR AND THE FIRST PLAYER TO WIN BATTING TITLES IN THREE DECADES (1976, '80, '90). HIT .390 IN 1980 MVP SEASON AND LED ROYALS TO FIRST WORLD SERIES TITLE IN 1985. RANKS AMONG ALL-TIME LEADERS IN HITS, DOUBLES, LONG HITS AND TOTAL BASES. A.L. CAREER RECORD, MOST INTENTIONAL WALKS. A CLUTCH HITTER WHOSE PROFOUND RESPECT FOR THE GAME LED TO UNIVERSAL REVERENCE.

Honus Wagner | Grover Cleveland Alexander | Tris Speaker | Napoleon Lajoie | George Sisler | Walter Johnson

Eddie Collins | Babe Ruth | Connie Mack | Cy Young

A GATHERING OF GREATNESS

In 1936, baseball began electing players and coaches to the Baseball Hall of Fame. The Hall itself didn't open until 1939, on the alleged 100th anniversary of baseball (the anniversary was based on the now-debunked theory that Abner Doubleday "invented" the game in 1839). This photograph of all the then-living Hall of Fame members was taken at the dedication. Ty Cobb was also at the event, but missed the photograph. The players, together with longtime Philadelphia owner and manager Connie Mack, make up one of the greatest assemblages of baseball talent ever seen in one place.

B for Brooklyn

JACKIE'S CAP

The Hall of Fame boasts an enormous collection of baseball caps, including this one worn by Dodgers' great Jackie Robinson. The collection includes caps from every era of pro and amateur baseball. When asked, players gladly donate their caps to the Hall to commemorate a special occasion.

Classic Yankee pinstripes

1956 WORLD SERIES AMERICAN LEAGUE VS NATIONAL LEAGUE

1956 WORLD SERIES American League / National League

GAME 5 ONLY — YANKEE STADIUM BOX SEAT $10.50 TAX INCLUDED
Do not detach this coupon from RAIN CHECK.

GAME 5 YANKEE STADIUM NEW YORK YANKEES Agent

RAIN CHECK RETAIN THIS CHECK Not Good If Detached ADMIT ONE—Subject to the conditions set forth on the back hereof. Played Under the Supervision of FORD C. FRICK Commissioner of Baseball

SECTION 26 ROW 178A BOX 1 SEAT 1

MEZZANINE BOX SEAT

ENTER AT GATE 2

TICKET TO HISTORY

This 1956 World Series ticket is an example of the Hall of Fame's vast resources on the paper record of baseball. Each season, the historians at the Hall add many more items to their collection of tickets, scorebooks, magazines, books, and newspaper articles.

CLASS OF 1999

The annual Hall of Fame induction ceremony is one of the greatest events of each baseball season. Inductees are presented in front of a crowd of thousands and give speeches broadcast nationwide thanking those who helped them reach the top. These four all-time great players were inducted in 1999.

DIRTY DIMAGGIO

One of the great hallmarks of the artifacts fans can see at the Hall of Fame is their authenticity. This jersey is one example. Worn by Yankee great Joe DiMaggio, it retains the sweat and dirt and grass stains that the "Yankee Clipper" put there himself. The artifacts aren't replicas—they're the real McCoy. Along with the hundreds of items on display, the Hall also carefully stores and preserves thousands of other pieces of baseball memorabilia, creating new exhibits each season that highlight different aspects of baseball's past.

Orlando Cepeda | Robin Yount | Nolan Ryan | George Brett

World Series History

THE HISTORY OF Major League Baseball can be traced almost completely by following the timeline of the World Series. The game's annual championship—played between the champions of the American and National Leagues—has become as much a part of America's calendar as the Fourth of July. The first Fall Classic, as it is sometimes called, was in

1903: Boston wins five games to three.

1903 (left), and it has been played every year—with one notable exception—since 1905. The exception? The 1994 World Series was canceled during a labor dispute between players and owners. Every other year, the World Series has gone on through war and peace and everything in between. While generations of baseball's greatest players have created indelible memories on the field (see page 56), the constant popularity of the World Series has helped create a colorful legacy of Series stuff, as shown on these pages.

THE BLACK SOX

The fan who used this ticket to the 1919 World Series between the Cincinnati Reds and the Chicago White Sox witnessed one of baseball's darkest hours. Eight members of the White Sox conspired with gamblers to throw the Series to the underdog Reds. The "Black Sox," as they came to be known, were later suspended from baseball for life. One of them, "Shoeless" Joe Jackson, was one of the greatest hitters of all time. There is debate bout Jackson's role in the fix, but there is no debate that the fix was in. Baseball's pure reputation had been tarnished.

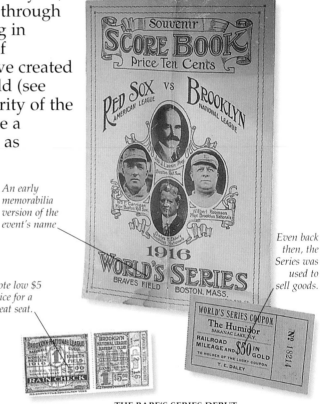

An early memorabilia version of the event's name

Even back then, the Series was used to sell goods.

PINNING DOWN THE WORLD SERIES

The now-popular hobby of collecting pins commemorating major sports events did not start with the Olympics. Pins such as the ones below have been issued for the World Series since the first games. An example from 1913 (below) shows an early version of the name of the event: "World's Series." The members of the press covering the Series have always enjoyed special pins, such as the ribbon in the center, issued in 1917 by the New York Giants, and the pin at upper left, issued by the American League in 1927.

From 1908, the year of the Giants' first Series appearance

New York Giants tie tack

Note low $5 price for a great seat.

Baseball premade for canceled 1994 Series

THE BABE'S SERIES DEBUT

The great Babe Ruth made his World Series debut in 1916, but he made his mark as a pitcher, not a hitter. Ruth's 14-inning, complete game, one-run victory in Game 2 proved to be the key to Boston's title. The Red Sox would win again with Ruth in 1918 for their fifth title in 15 seasons. Ruth left the next season, and Boston hasn't won a Series since.

THE SERIES THAT WASN'T

Disagreements between owners and players have been a part of baseball since the 1860s. The worst example of baseball labor problems came in 1994. Amid an ongoing battle over salaries, the players went on strike on August 12 that year, and they didn't return until 1995. For the only time in the history of the event, the World Series was canceled.

THE RIVALRY

For decades, the Brooklyn Dodgers and New York Yankees were fierce crosstown rivals, facing each other seven times in the World Series; Brooklyn won only in 1955. The Dodgers moved to Los Angeles in 1959. In 1963, they swept the Yankees in the Series, winning in L.A. on the strength of pitcher Sandy Koufax's magical left arm.

Pennants representing each major league team

A TRIP TO THE WHITE HOUSE
Since baseball is America's pastime, it is only fitting that an annual ritual is for the World Series champions to pay a visit to the White House to meet the President soon after they win the title.

President George W. Bush met with manager Mike Scoscia of the 2002 champion Angels.

CHAMPAGNE DREAMS COME TRUE
Until recently, after the final game of each World Series, the commissioner of baseball visited the locker room of the jubilant winning team to present this trophy to the team owners and manager. Recently, to make the presentation more fan-friendly, the ceremony has moved to a stage hastily built on the field amid the celebrating players and fans. What once was a champagne-soaked party in cramped, plastic-covered quarters has now sometimes become a field-spanning spectacle of fireworks, frivolity, and fun. Players race across the field to hug each other; they bring their children down from the stands; they climb on top of police horses for triumphant parades. All the while, a stadium full of fans—and millions more watching on TV—bears witness to the unbridled joy of victory.

Newly-designed trophy debuted with the 2000 World Series, won by the Yankees.

DRINK OF CHAMPIONS
Most Series souvenirs are traditional, such as pennants, hats, and shirts. But there's always room for things like this commemorative soda.

THE MIGHTY YANKEES
The New York Yankees have dominated the World Series like no other team. The Bronx Bombers have appeared in 37 World Series and won 26 times, more than twice as many as their nearest rivals, the Athletics and Cardinals (who have won nine Series apiece). The Yankees won their first World Series in 1923. Their most recent championship was in 2000 (below). This pennant is from their 1998 championship. They are the only team to win four World Series in a row (1936–39), and the only team to win five in a row (1949–53). They won at least one title in every decade except the 1980s.

RINGING IN THE TITLE
While the World Series trophy resides in the winning team's offices, the players' symbol of victory is the World Series ring. This model, from the 1954 New York Giants, shows an early example. Recent rings are enormous, with many diamonds.

Yankees' famous top hat logo

World Series Heroes

Two outs, bottom of the ninth, seventh game of the World Series. Your team is behind, and it's all up to you. Can you save the day? For nearly 100 years, kids across America have played that scene in their minds and in their schoolyard games. Can you make the big hit and win the Series? Can you be a hero? When it came time for the men on these pages to ask that question of themselves, to face the great pressure of the World Series—whether bottom of the ninth or earlier—they all answered, "Yes, I can!" Like the kids they all once were, it was a dream come true.

A-MAZ-ING
Until 1960, no team had earned its World Series title by hitting a home run on the final swing of the Series. Then along came Bill Mazeroski. The Pirates' second baseman, known more for his outstanding fielding than his hitting, led off the bottom of the ninth with the Yankees and Pirates tied 9-9 in Game 7. Maz slugged a home run into the left field seats for a shocking 10-9 victory over the Yankees.

PITCHER PERFECT
On baseball's biggest stage, no pitcher was ever better for one game than Don Larsen. In the fifth game of the 1956 World Series, the Yankees right-hander threw the only perfect game in World Series history, and one of only 17 such games in all of baseball since 1880. Larsen, here being congratulated by catcher Yogi Berra, faced 27 Brooklyn Dodgers and retired them all. Not one Dodger reached first base.

Larsen's career record was 81-91.

THE YANKEE CLIPPER
Yankees center fielder Joe DiMaggio never won a World Series with a homer or made a Series-winning catch. He just won. In 13 seasons (1936-51) with the Yankees, DiMaggio led the team to 10 World Series titles. His clutch hitting (he had 30 RBI in 51 games), graceful fielding, and quiet leadership were the keystones to the great Yankees teams of the 1930s and 1940s. DiMaggio, who died in 1999, became an enduring symbol of the Yankees' dynasty.

GIMPY GIBBY
Although it came in Game 1 of the 1998 World Series, not Game 7, a dramatic two-run homer by injured and limping Kirk Gibson in the bottom of the ninth gave the Los Angeles Dodgers the lift they needed to upset the favored Oakland A's for the Series title.

A GREAT MAN ON AND OFF THE FIELD
In the 1971 World Series, Roberto Clemente, the pride of Puerto Rico, hit .414 while reaching base safely in all seven games. His home run in Game 7 proved decisive as the Pirates defeated the Orioles 2-1 to win the Series. Clemente's final Series appearance was bittersweet. Following the 1972 season, when he reached 3,000 career hits in his last game, Clemente was tragically killed in a plane crash while helping deliver supplies to earthquake victims in Nicaragua.

In 1941, DiMaggio hit safely in a record 56 consecutive games.

Jackson is fifth all-time with 10 Series home runs.

CARTER'S CLOUT
Toronto outfielder Joe Carter leaps for joy as he watches his World Series-winning homer leave the yard in 1993's Game 6. The three-run blast brought the Blue Jays from a run behind. They won the game 8-6 and the Series 4-2 over the Philadelphia Phillies.

MISTER OCTOBER
Few players in baseball history have craved the limelight Reginald Martinez Jackson. Reggie Jackson earned his nickname of "Mister October" with a string of clutch hits in World Series games for Oakland and New York. But it was in Game 6 of the 1977 World Series that he carved a permanent place in baseball lore. Jackson blasted home runs on three consecutive pitches from Dodgers hurlers. Only Babe Ruth, who did it twice, has also homered three times in a Series game.

Fisk's bat

FISK AND FENWAY
Red Sox catcher Carlton Fisk ended what many call the greatest game in Series history—Game 6 in 1975—with a home run in the bottom of the twelfth inning. Fisk's homer over Fenway Park's "Green Monster" gave Boston a 7-6 victory.

Jackson had 563 career home runs.

The Home Run

Aaron broke in with the Milwaukee Braves, who later moved to Atlanta.

FOUR-BAGGER. Circuit clout. Round-tripper. Dinger. Tater. Quadrangular. Homer. By any name, the home run is baseball's signature moment. Sock the ball out of the yard and you render the other team helpless. There is no defense for a home run. And nothing energizes a crowd or a team like a well-timed shot to the seats. All of baseball's greatest heroes are home run hitters. The Babe. Larrupin' Lou. Old Double X. The Mick. Say-Hey Willie. Hammerin' Hank. Big Mac. The frenzy created by Mark McGwire and Sammy Sosa as they chased history and each other throughout 1998 wouldn't have happened if they had been chasing the record for doubles. Purists can argue that home runs are overvalued and that players ruin their swings aiming for the fences instead of the gaps. But here's a guarantee: All of those purists are on their feet yelling along with the rest of us as a record-setting or World Series-winning home run soars through the sky into history. Backbackbackback! Going, going, gone! Good-bye, Mr. Spalding! It might be, it could be, it is…a home run!

HAMMERIN' HANK
On April 8, 1974, Hank Aaron broke a record many thought was unbreakable. The Braves outfielder, shown here early in his career, hit his 715th career home run, breaking the mark set by the immortal Babe Ruth. Aaron, who finished his career in 1976 with 755 homers, suffered through racist threats as he approached Ruth's mark. But his class and talent overcame the bigotry. Sadly, Aaron remains one of the sports world's least appreciated superstars.

THE SHOT HEARD 'ROUND THE WORLD
Giants outfielder Bobby Thompson hit one of baseball's most famous home runs, a three-run shot in the bottom of the ninth that gave the Giants the 1951 National League championship over the Brooklyn Dodgers.

Thomson earned a hug from Giants manager Leo Durocher (left).

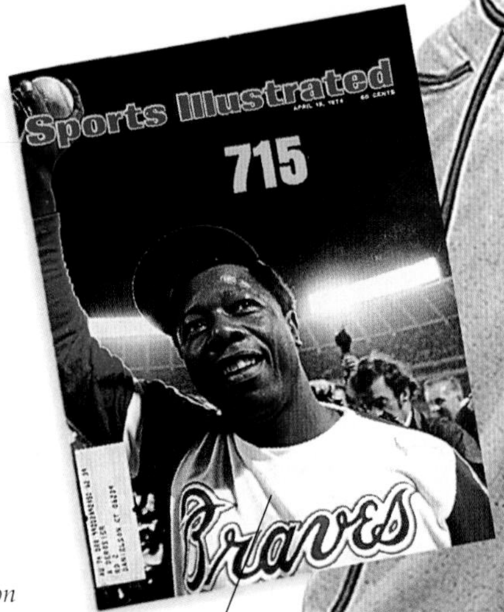

No words were needed when Aaron set the record.

Compare the baggy pants worn by Aaron in 1961 with the sleek outfits of McGwire and Sosa (right).

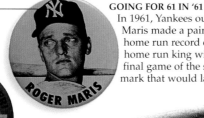

ROGER MARIS

A September, 1961, knee injury ended Mantle's chase.

GOING FOR 61 IN '61
In 1961, Yankees outfielders Mickey Mantle and Roger Maris made a paired assault on Ruth's single-season home run record of 60. Maris became the new home run king with his 61st homer in the final game of the season, setting a mark that would last until 1998.

THE MIGHTY MICK
With 536 home runs, Mickey Mantle is eighth all-time. But there is more to Mantle's home run story than a number. He holds the career record for World Series home runs with 18, hitting them when his team needed them most. He holds the record for most homers by a switch-hitter, showing his power from both sides of the plate. And he hit what has been called the longest home-run ever, a mammoth 565-foot blast in 1952 in Washington's Griffith Stadium. If not for his constant injury problems, Mantle may have caught the Babe, too.

McGwire's bat is now in the Hall of Fame.

Mantle underwent several knee surgeries.

Mantle's speed and Oklahoma hometown earned him his nickname: The Commerce Comet.

RECORD BREAKER
With this mighty swing on September 8, 1998, Cardinals first baseman Mark McGwire hit his major-league record 62nd home run of the season, capping off a remarkable chase of the mark of 61 set by Roger Maris in 1961. An entire nation of fans followed Big Mac's every at-bat throughout the summer as he neared the magic number. But while McGwire's moon-shot power was the cause of all the fuss (he ended the season with an amazing 70 homers), it was his class, style, and grace under pressure that made the summer of '98 so special.

McGwire wore a plastic guard on his ankle to guard against foul tips.

QUITE A NICKNAME
Frank "Home Run" Baker (far right) earned his famous nickname by reaching double digits in home runs five times in a "dead-ball" era when some teams did not hit 10 homers in a season.

BLASTING INTO HISTORY
Amazingly, only three years after McGwire's record-setting year, San Francisco's Barry Bonds topped Big Mac. The lefty Giants slugger whacked a stunning 73 home runs in 2002. And he just kept going. In 2004, he became only the third player in baseball history (along with Hank Aaron and Babe Ruth) to exceed 700 career home runs.

Did you know?

Jim Abbott

Pitcher Jim Abbott (above) was born without a right hand, but still became a successful Major Leaguer. On September 4, 1993, Jim pitched a no-hitter for the New York Yankees against the Cleveland Indians at Yankee Stadium.

Joe DiMaggio's streak of hitting safely in 56 consecutive games began on May 15, 1941. Over the next two months, he had at least one base hit in every game in which he played. During that time, he batted .408 with 15 home runs and 55 runs batted in. The streak finally ended on July 17, 1941, against the Cleveland Indians. DiMaggio reached safely in the next 16 games, making his streak 72 out of 73 games.

Dummy Hoy played the outfield for six teams from 1888 to 1902 and had a lifetime batting average of .288. That was not good enough to get him to the Hall of Fame, but he did leave his mark in another way. Dummy Hoy was the first deaf baseball player. Because of his hearing impairment, umpires began to use hand signals to call balls and strikes.

On April 29, 1986, Roger Clemens of the Boston Red Sox set a major league record by striking out 20 batters in a nine-inning game. Roger didn't walk a single batter during the game. He gave up three hits and got the win as the Red Sox defeated the Seattle Mariners, 3-1, at Fenway Park. Clemens struck out 20 for a second time in September 1996.

Mario Mendoza was a slick-fielding but dreadfully weak-hitting shortstop for the Seattle Mariners. When he hit .198 as a regular in 1979, teammates began referring to .200 as the "Mendoza Line." Soon major league players stopped saying that a player couldn't hit his weight; now an unsuccessful hitter had sunk "below the Mendoza Line."

Singing the song "Take Me Out To The Ballgame" (right) is tradition during the seventh-inning stretch. The song was written in 1908 by Jack Norworth and Harry von Tilzer. At the time, neither man had ever seen a baseball game!

Only 11 players in major-league history have won the Triple Crown, which means they led their league in home runs, RBIs, and batting average during the same season. The last to do it was Carl Yastrzemski of the Boston Red Sox, in 1967. Two players won the Triple Crown twice: Rogers Hornsby of the St. Louis Cardinals (in 1922 and 1925) and Ted Williams of the Red Sox (in 1943 and 1947).

The longest home run on record was a 565-foot clout hit at old Griffith Stadium on April 17, 1953. Mickey Mantle, a switch-hitter for the New York Yankees, was batting righthanded against lefthanded pitcher Chuck Stobbs of the Washington Senators. Mantle hit a rising line drive that left the stadium, carried across the street, and landed in the back yard of a home.

By joining the Seattle Mariners in 1989, Ken Griffey Jr. made history. Ken Sr. and Ken Jr. (right) became the first father and son to play in the major leagues at the same time. And one year later, they appeared in the same lineup, when the Mariners signed Ken Sr. On September 14, 1990, they hit back-to-back homers!

A memorable All-Star Game moment occurred in the 1934 game, when National League pitcher Carl Hubbell of the New York Giants struck out five future Hall of Famers in a row: Babe Ruth, Lou Gehrig, Jimmie Foxx, Al Simmons, and Joe Cronin. Hubbell himself was eventually inducted into the Hall of Fame.

In 2004, Los Angeles Dodgers Robin Ventura and Olmedo Saenz became the first teammates with pinch-hit grand slams in consecutive games.

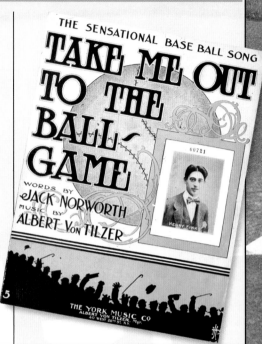

THE SENSATIONAL BASE BALL SONG

TAKE ME OUT TO THE BALL GAME

WORDS BY JACK NORWORTH
MUSIC BY ALBERT VON TILZER

HARRY FINK

THE YORK MUSIC CO.
ALBERT VON TILZER, Mgr.
40 WEST 28TH ST. N.Y.

"Take Me Out to the Ballgame" song sheet

The 2004 Texas Rangers became the first team since 1950 to boast four infielders with 20 or more homers: Hank Blalock (3B), Michael Young (SS), Alfonso Soriano (2B), and Mark Teixeira (1B).

The Roberto Clemente Award was established in 1971 to honor the late Hall of Fame Pirates outfielder, who was killed in a plane crash while bringing relief supplies to earthquake victims. It is given to a player devoted to great community service.

Ken Griffey Sr. and Ken Griffey Jr.

QUESTIONS AND ANSWERS

Q What two players together hold the all-time record for home runs by a pair of brothers?

A It's kind of a trick question: Hank Aaron had 755, while his brother Tommy had 13!

Q When was the first pro baseball game aired on television?

A August 22, 1939; a game between the Brooklyn Dodgers and Cincinnati Reds was shown on TV in New York City.

Q What was the last Major League ballpark to go without lights?

A Until 1988, Chicago's Wrigley Field did not have lights; the Cubs played all their home games in the daytime. Even after lights were installed, they play the majority of their games in daylight.

Q What little-known record did Seattle's Ichiro Suzuki break in 2004?

A On his way to an amazing total of 262 hits, Ichiro smacked 225 singles, topping the old mark of 198 set by Lloyd Waner.

Q The batter hits a long fly ball that bounces on the field in fair territory and then lands untouched over the fence or into the stands. What is the umpire's call?

A Ground rule double. The batter must stop at second base.

A baserunner tries to avoid the tag during a rundown.

Q Who are the Bronx Bombers, the Pale Hose, and the Friars?

A Those are nicknames for the New York Yankees, Chicago White Sox, and San Diego Padres, respectively.

Q Who were Big Poison and Little Poison, Dizzy and Daffy, and Tony C and Billy C?

A Those are nicknames for three pairs of baseball brothers: Lloyd and Paul Waner; Jay and Paul Dean; and Tony and Billy Conigliaro.

Q A fielder with the ball in his possession tags a runner leading off second base while the pitcher is not on the mound. What is the umpire's call?

A The runner is out. This is often called the "hidden-ball trick"; it is only legal when the pitcher is not standing on the mound.

Q What is a "can of corn"?

A An easy fly ball. The term comes from when old-time grocers used their aprons to catch cans knocked from a high shelf.

Q What two Hall of Fame catchers won a total of six MVP awards in the 1950s?

A The Yankees' Yogi Berra was the A.L. MVP in 1951, '54, and '55. Brooklyn Dodgers' star Roy Campanella was the N.L. MVP in 1951, '53, and '55.

Ichiro Suzuki does a drag bunt.

Q What is the Hank Aaron Award?

A First given in 2000, this award goes to the best hitter, statistically, in each league. It is named, of course, after Aaron, baseball's all-time home-run king with 755 career homers. He is also the all-time leader in runs batted in with 2,297.

Q A base runner is caught in a rundown. The infielder holds the ball in his bare hand and tags the runner with his glove before he reaches the base. What is the umpire's call?

A The runner is safe. A fielder must tag the runner with the ball.

Q Who threw the first no-hitter?

A Appropriately, George Washington Bradley tossed the first one for the St. Louis Brown Stockings in 1876.

Baseball Math

Batting average

The number of hits divided by the number of at-bats. Example: A batter with 7 hits in 21 at-bats has a .333 batting average; this is calculated as 7 (hits) divided by 21 (at-bats). You can do the same to figure out a player's career or season average. A player with an average above .300 is considered a high-quality hitter.

Earned run average (E.R.A.)

The average number of earned runs a pitcher allows in a nine-inning game. Calculated as the earned runs multiplied by nine and then divided by the number of innings pitched; example: A pitcher who allows 10 earned runs in 30 innings pitched has an ERA of 3.00; this is calculated as 10 (earned runs) times 9 (innings per game), which equals 90, divided by 30 (innings pitched).

On-base percentage

A batter's number of hits plus walks plus times hit by a pitch divided by the number of official at-bats plus walks plus times hit by a pitch plus sacrifices. Example: A batter with five hits and one walk in 11 official at-bats has a .500 on-base percentage (five hits plus one walk divided by 11 at-bats plus one walk).

Slugging percentage

This is calculated by dividing the total number of bases a player has reached on singles, doubles (the number of doubles times two), triples (the number of triples times three), and home runs (the number of home runs times four) by his number of times at-bat. Example: A player with one HR and one 2B in 10 ABs has six total bases in 10 at bats for a .600 slugging percentage.

Baseball Calendar

MAJOR LEAGUE BASEBALL'S regular season goes from April through October. But baseball has become a year-round game. Here are some events to watch in a year of baseball.

FEBRUARY AND MARCH

Spring Training. Pitchers and catchers report first, about two weeks before the position players. Teams training in Florida make up what is called the "Grapefruit League." Teams training in Arizona play in the "Cactus League."

APRIL

Opening Day. Celebrations take place in stadiums throughout both leagues, the highlight of which is the ceremonial first pitch, often by a celebrity or politician, such as the president of the United States.

JUNE

College World Series. College teams from around the nation compete in Omaha, Nebraska, at Rosenblatt Stadium, host of the College World Series since 1964.

First-Year Player Draft. The Major League Baseball draft of high school and college players is held by conference call among the 30 major league clubs. Beginning in 2005, clubs will select in reverse order of winning percentage, regardless of league.

Hall Of Fame Game. This annual exhibition game is played between two Major League clubs at Doubleday Field in Cooperstown, New York. It is a great treat for fans, but it does not count in the regular season standings.

JULY

All-Star Game. The best players in the National and American Leagues compete in this game, held in a different big-league city every year since 1933. The starting position players are chosen by fans, who vote using official ballots. Pitchers and substitutes are chosen by the managers of the two teams that played in the World Series the previous year. Starting in 2003, the winning team earned home-field advantage for its league in the World Series.

Hall Of Fame Induction ceremony. Players become eligible for the Hall five years after they retire. They are chosen by the Baseball Writers Association of America. There is also a special veterans committee that chooses worthy players who have been overlooked by the writers.

Trading deadline. From the end of the season until August, Major League teams can trade players to help build their lineups. Starting in August, however, players need to clear waivers before they can be traded. A player on waivers can be claimed by any other team, which must purchase that player's contract.

Opening Day is always a baseball fan's favorite day of the year.

AUGUST

Little League World Series. Teams from all over the world compete in this tournament, held in Williamsport, Pennsylvania, each summer since 1947. The final game is broadcast on national television. Little League has many age divisions, but this World Series is for the top teams of 11–12 year olds. Both boys and girls can play Little League at most levels.

All-Star players wear caps with a special patch.

SEPTEMBER

Major league rosters expand from 25 players to 40, giving numerous minor leaguers their first taste of the big leagues.

OCTOBER

The regular season ends near the beginning of the month, and the postseason begins.

Division Series: The three first-place teams and one wild-card team from each league face off in the Division Series. The League Championship Series are between the Division Series winners.

Frankie Rodriguez in the All-Star Game

World Series: Since 1903, this series has determined the Major League Baseball champion. The LCS winners play in a best-of-seven series. The format usually has the two league champions meet for two games in the "home" city (see All-Star Game, above), then three games in the other city, and returning for two more in the home city, if necessary.

NOVEMBER

Post-season awards. After each season, members of the Baseball Writers Association of America vote for the players and pitchers they feel were the best in each league. The major awards are Most Valuable Player, Rookie of the Year, Cy Young Award, Manager of the Year, and Glove Gloves for fielding excellence.

DECEMBER

Winter Meetings. This is an annual conference when owners, team executives, and player representatives meet to discuss the state of the game and possible rule changes. Many blockbuster trades also occur during these meetings, which are held in a different city each year. Then it's just a few long weeks until Spring Training starts again!

Making The Majors

MAJOR LEAGUE BASEBALL players have worked hard and beaten the odds. According to the National Collegiate Athletic Association (NCAA), about 5.6 percent of high school baseball players will go on to play men's baseball at an NCAA college. About 10.5 percent of NCAA players will get drafted by a Major League Baseball team. Plus, only about 0.5 percent of high school players will eventually be drafted by an MLB team. The talented few who are drafted must start at the bottom and work their way up. So get started soon!

Milwaukee prospect Rickie Weeks

Summer Baseball

Former pros looking to keep their baseball dreams alive and current college players just starting out on their careers take part in a large number of summer baseball leagues. Around the country—including Alaska, Cape Cod, Michigan, Texas, Kansas, and California—players use wood bats (college players normally play with aluminum bats) to play in front of small-town crowds.

2003 national champion Santa Barbara Foresters

Minor League Baseball

Minor league baseball is like a ladder with each rung taking a player closer and closer to the Majors.

ROOKIE BALL
Appalachian League
Arizona League
Pioneer League
Gulf Coast League

CLASS A
California League
Midwest League

Carolina League
South Atlantic League
Florida State League

CLASS A
SHORT SEASON
New York-Penn League
Northwest League

DOUBLE A
Eastern League
Southern League
Texas League

TRIPLE A
International League
Pacific Coast League

College Baseball

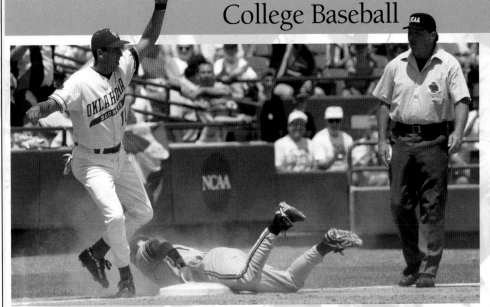

The dust flies at the annual College World Series, held annually in Omaha, Nebraska.

Colleges of all shapes and sizes field baseball teams. The highest level of college ball is called Division I. There are more than 280 colleges and universities in Division I. Smaller colleges compete in the Division II and Division III levels. There are championship tournaments for all three divisions. Baseball is also played at many two-year schools, such as junior colleges or community colleges. College players can be selected to join pro leagues after their freshman or junior seasons. These players then join a Major League organization.

Find out more

WE HOPE *Eyewitness Baseball* has sparked your interest in baseball. On these pages are some ways you can find more information about your favorite players and teams. Visit Web sites, read books, stop by the ballparks, or collect autographs. There are many ways that you can keep baseball as a part of your life all year 'round!

Bring your own pen to get autographs.

SIGN MY BALL, PLEASE!
When you get to meet a real big-league star in person (like these kids, who are meeting Dodgers' first baseman Hee Seop Choi), ask politely for an autograph. Make sure to have a pen and something to sign and be patient and polite. The only times on game days that players may be able to sign in person is before the game, usually after they have completed batting practice. This can be as much as two hours before a game. Call ahead to find out when the entry gates are opened before games at your ballpark.

MAYBE I'LL BE UP THERE SOMEDAY
The highlight of every trip to the Baseball Hall of Fame in Cooperstown, New York, is a visit to the hall of plaques honoring the members of the Hall. These visitors check out the brass plaques saluting the first five players chosen for the Hall in 1936: Babe Ruth, Honus Wagner, Ty Cobb, Walter Johnson, and Christy Mathewson. New plaques are put up each summer following induction ceremonies attended by tens of thousands of fans. You can also check out thousands of pieces of famous gear like this Brooklyn Dodgers cap worn by Hall of Famer Jackie Robinson.

USEFUL WEB SITES

www.mlb.com
The official Web site of Major League Baseball is packed with information about all the teams and players. Complete season and career stats can be checked, along with historical stats of thousands of former players. Watch video, listen to games, order gear, and much more.

www.baseballhalloffame.org
Read about all the members of the Baseball Hall of Fame on this official site. Also includes photos of hundreds of pieces of historic memorabilia.

www.littleleague.org
Find out where you can play in your area or read about the annual Little League World Series. There are leagues for all ages and genders.

www.espn.com/mlb
This site from one of MLB's official television partners features in-depth scouting reports and articles by top national baseball writers.

READ ALL ABOUT IT!
Your local library or bookstore has hundreds of books about baseball. Some examples are shown here, including *Play Ball: The Official MLB Guide for Young Players*. You can learn all the techniques you'll need to play the game. Other books tell you about the history of the game, about great individual performances, or about memorable moments. Readers at all levels will find both fiction and nonfiction about baseball. Ask about baseball videos and DVDs, too.

CAUTION: KIDS HAVING FUN

Little League Baseball is the oldest and largest international youth baseball organization. It started in 1939 in Pennsylvania and now has teams in more than 100 countries. The children in red above are from the Caribbean island of Curacao; they have just won the 2004 Little League World Series championship. Whether in Little League or some other youth baseball group, join up and "Play ball." Ask your parents to check with your local parks and recreation department or check the phone book for baseball leagues in your area. You can also find baseball schools where you can practice your skills. A trip to a batting cage is a fun way to work on hitting, too.

Places to Visit

NATIONAL BASEBALL HALL OF FAME AND LIBRARY
Located in Cooperstown, New York, this shrine to baseball's past includes thousands of one-of-a-kind artifacts from heroes past and present. The highlight is the room where the more than 200 Hall of Fame members' plaques are displayed.

NEGRO LEAGUE BASEBALL MUSEUM
Learn more about this important part of baseball history. Read about great players, see the gear they used, and watch special video presentations. This museum is located in Kansas City, Missouri.

YANKEE STADIUM
The home of the New York Yankees has been the site of perhaps more baseball memories than any other park. A special treat is a visit to Monument Park behind left field, which honors heroes from the Yankees.

FENWAY PARK
The home of the Boston Red Sox is a treat for fans of any team. The oldest park still in use in the Majors, Fenway features an enormous green left-field wall known as "The Monster." Fenway's location right in the middle of the city makes it a trip back to baseball's past.

WRIGLEY FIELD
The Chicago Cubs' home features real ivy growing on its famous brick outfield walls. Check out the seats on the roofs of buildings behind the outfield walls!

ROSENBLATT STADIUM
The Omaha, Nebraska, home of the college baseball World Series showcases the great players who have played there.

GO THE BALLPARK!

Cincinnati Reds' reliever Danny Graves knows the best place to hang out with his kids: At the ballpark. Whether you go to a Major League park, a Minor League park, a college game, a high school game, or even a youth baseball game, there's nothing quite like watching baseball in person. The smell of the grass, the crack (or ping!) of the bat, the thwack of the ball into leather gloves—it's a huge part of summer for millions. Look in your local phone book or newspaper to find out where you can go see a game in your area.

Glossary

ASSIST Statistic credited to fielders when they throw runners out

BACKSTOP A high fence behind home plate that protects spectators and keeps batted or thrown balls within the field of play; also a slang term for the catcher

BALK If a pitcher tries to deceive a base runner after placing his foot on the pitcher's rubber, the umpire will call a balk; all runners advance one base.

BALL Any pitch outside the strike zone at which a batter does not swing

BASE RUNNER A player who safely reaches base

BATTER An offensive player who comes up to home plate to try to get on base

BATTER'S BOX The six-foot by four-foot rectangle on each side of home plate in which batters must stand when hitting

BATTING AVERAGE The number of hits divided by the number of at-bats. Example: A batter with seven hits in 21 at-bats has a .333 batting average.

BOX SCORE A detailed summary of statistics from a particular game in box form

BULLPEN The area where pitchers warm up before and during games; usually located behind the outfield wall

BUNT A soft hit resulting from the batter holding the bat out and letting the ball hit it instead of swinging the bat. A batter sometimes will give himself up to advance a base runner by bunting; this is called a sacrifice bunt.

CATCHER A defensive player who plays behind home plate and receives pitches from the pitcher

CENTER FIELDER A defensive player who is positioned in the center of the outfield

CHANGE-UP A slow pitch that is usually thrown after several fast ones to throw off the timing of a batter's swing. A pitcher who throws a successful change-up is said to "pull the string."

COMPLETE GAME A game in which a pitcher pitches every inning

CURVEBALL A pitch that curves as it reaches the plate. It is thrown by snapping the wrist

Curveball grip

sharply away from the body as the pitch is released, so the ball spins rapidly and veers to the left (if thrown with the right hand) or right (if thrown with the left hand). Also known as a breaking ball, hook, bender, or biter.

DIAMOND Another word for the infield

DOUBLE A hit on which the batter reaches second base safely. Also known as a two-bagger

DOUBLEHEADER When the same two teams play two games on the same date; also called a twin bill

DOUBLE PLAY When two outs are made by the defense during one play. Known by the offense as a "twin killing"; by the defense as the "pitcher's best friend."

DOUBLE STEAL A play in which two runners attempt to steal bases at the same time

EARNED RUN A run scored because of a hit, hit batsman, or walk that is charged to a pitcher's earned run average (ERA). Runs that score because of errors are unearned.

EARNED RUN AVERAGE (ERA) The average number of earned runs a pitcher allows in a nine-inning game. It is calculated as a pitcher's earned runs allowed multiplied by nine and then divided by the number of innings pitched. Example: A pitcher who allows 10 earned runs in 30 innings pitched has an ERA of 3.00.

ERROR A misplay by a fielder that allows a runner to reach base safely or score; also called a bobble or a muff

FAIR TERRITORY Any part of the playing field within the baselines

FASTBALL A straight pitch that is thrown with maximum speed and power. A fastball pitcher with a great "heater" is said to be "throwing smoke." Also called "high cheese."

FIRST BASEMAN A defensive player who is positioned on the right side of the infield near first base; also called the first sacker

FLY BALL A ball hit high in the air. A short fly ball also is called a popup.

FORCE PLAY A play in which the base runner must try to advance to the next base on a batted ball. On a force play, a fielder with the ball may register an out by touching the base ahead of the runner instead of having to tag him.

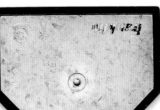

Home plate

Torii Hunter stands in as a batter.

FOUL TERRITORY Any part of the playing field outside of the baselines

GRAND SLAM A home run with the bases loaded; also called a grand salami (slang)

GROUND BALL A hit ball that rolls or bounces on the ground; a grounder; also called a grass cutter or a worm burner (slang)

GROUND-RULE DOUBLE When a batter is awarded two bases on a hit that lands in fair territory and bounces over the fence or is interfered with by fans

HOME PLATE A rubber slab at which the batter stands to receive pitches. A batter must start and end a trip around the bases at home plate. Also called the dish (slang).

HOME RUN A four-base hit on which the batter scores a run for his team. Balls traveling over the fence are also called a four-bagger, round-tripper, fence-clearer, dinger, tater, jack, belt, long ball, bomb, moon shot, rain maker, clout, big bash, big fly, big swat, wallop, slam or smash. The hitter is said to go yard, go downtown, touch 'em all, unload one, go deep, park it, or get all of it. A pitcher who gives up a home run is said to throw a "gopher ball."

INFIELD The part of the field close to home plate that contains the bases; also called a diamond

INNING A segment of a baseball game in which each team has a turn at bat. Major league games are nine innings, while most youth baseball games are six innings.

Catcher's mitt

MITT Another term for a fielder's glove, especially those worn by first basemen (whose mitts have elongated webbing for catching throws) or catchers (whose mitts have extra padding for catching pitches)

NO-HITTER When a pitcher or pitchers on the same team do not allow a base hit during a game

ON-BASE PERCENTAGE A batter's total number of hits plus walks plus times hit by a pitch, divided by the number of at-bats plus walks plus times hit by a pitch plus sacrifices

OUTFIELD The large, grassy area beyond the infield

PASSED BALL When a catcher fails to stop a pitch he should have caught, allowing a base runner to advance. If a passed ball comes on a third strike, the batter can run to first.

PEPPER A pre-game exercise in which one player hits brisk grounders and line drives to a group of fielders who are standing about 20 feet away. The fielders try to catch the ball and throw it back as quickly as possible. The batter hits the return throw.

PERFECT GAME A game in which a pitcher pitches every inning and does not let a runner reach base

PITCH A throw by the pitcher to a batter

Randy Johnson, Diamondbacks pitcher

PITCHER A defensive player whose job is to throw the baseball across home plate in an attempt to get the batter out. Pitchers stand on the mound at the center of the infield. They use a variety of types of throws when pitching.

PUTOUT A fielder is credited with a putout for catching a fly ball, pop-up, line drive, or throw that gets an opposing player out. A catcher receives a putout for catching a strikeout.

RIGHT FIELDER A defensive player who is positioned on the right side of the outfield

ROOKIE A player in his first season

RUNDOWN A base runner trapped by the defense while between two bases, being chased back and forth, before either being put out or reaching a base safely. A runner caught in this unenviable position is said to be "in a pickle."

SACRIFICE A bunt or fly ball that allows a runner to score or advance to another base at the expense of the batter, who is out

SAVE A pitcher gets credit for a save by finishing a close game while protecting his team's lead. If his team has a big lead, he can get a save by pitching the last three innings.

SCREWBALL A pitch that usually curves in toward a batter. A pitcher throws it by snapping his wrist in the direction of his body.

SECOND BASE A defensive player who is positioned on the right side of the infield between first base and second base

SHORTSTOP A defensive player who is positioned on the left side of the infield between second base and third base

SHUTOUT A pitcher who completes a game without allowing a run to the opposition is credited with a shutout. It also refers to a team that loses a game without scoring.

SINGLE A one-base hit; also called a base knock or bingle

SLIDER A pitch that is gripped more loosely than a curveball so that the ball "slides" out of the pitcher's hand. It looks like a fastball but curves sharply just as it reaches the plate.

STOLEN BASE A base gained by advancing when a batter does not hit a pitch

STRIKE Any pitch that passes through the strike zone or at which a batter swings and misses. An uncaught foul ball with fewer than two strikes also is a strike, as is a fouled bunt attempt (even with two strikes) and a foul tip (if with two strikes, it must be caught by the catcher to result in a third strike). A ball bunted foul after two strikes results in a strikeout.

STRIKEOUT An out recorded when a pitcher delivers three strikes (including foul balls) to a batter during an at-bat

STRIKE ZONE The area over the plate from the batter's knees up to the midpoint between the top of his uniform pants and shoulders. If a pitch passes through this area and the batter doesn't swing, the umpire calls a strike.

TAG To touch a player with the ball for an out. The ball can be in the fielder's hand or held inside his glove.

Rafael Furcal lays down a sacrifice bunt.

TAGGING UP Returning to touch base after a fly ball is caught for an out. Baserunners must wait until the ball has been caught before leaving a base to advance to the next open base or to score.

THIRD BASEMAN A defensive player who is positioned on the left side of the infield near third base. This area is known as the "hot corner."

TRIPLE A three-base hit; also known as a three-bagger

WALK A free trip to first base is awarded to a batter after a pitcher has issued four balls during one at-bat. A walk is symbolized by the letters BB in scoring, for "base on balls."

Strike zone

Team contact information

WANT TO LEARN MORE about your favorite team, write letters to your favorite players, or find out how to get tickets? Here are the addresses and phone numbers of the 30 Major League Baseball teams. Also listed are official team Web sites, or you can visit majorleaguebaseball.com. (Remember: Players receive thousands of letters every week, so yours may not get answered right away.)

AMERICAN LEAGUE

ANAHEIM ANGELS
EDISON FIELD
2000 Gene Autry Way
Anaheim, CA 92806
Phone: (714) 940-2000
www.angelsbaseball.com

BALTIMORE ORIOLES
ORIOLE PARK AT CAMDEN YARDS
333 West Camden Street
Baltimore, MD 21201
Phone: (888) 848-BIRD
www.theorioles.com

BOSTON RED SOX
FENWAY PARK
4 Yawkey Way
Boston, MA 02115-3496
Phone (617) 267-9440
www.redsox.com

CHICAGO WHITE SOX
U.S. CELULAR FIELD
333. W. 35th Street
Chicago, IL 60616
Phone: (312) 674-1000
www.chisox.com

CLEVELAND INDIANS
JACOBS FIELD
2401 Ontario Street
Cleveland, OH 44115
Phone: (216) 420-4200
www.indians.com

DETROIT TIGERS
COMERCIA PARK
2100 Woodward Avenue
Detroit, MI 48216
Phone: (313) 962-4000
www.detroittigers.com

KANSAS CITY ROYALS
KAUFFMAN STADIUM
P.O. Box 4199691
Kansas City, MO 64141-6969
Phone: (816) 921-8000
www.kcroyals.com

MINNESODA TWINS
METRODOME
34 Kirby Puckett Place
Minneapolis, MN 55415
Phone: (612) 375-1366
www.mntwins.com

NEW YORK YANKEES
YANKEE STADIUM
161st Street and River Avenue
Bronx, NY 10451
Phone: (718) 293-4300
www.yankees.com

OAKLAND ATHLETICS
NETWORK ASSOCIATES COLISEUM
7000 Coliseum Way
Oakland, CA 94621
Phone: (510) 569-2121
www.oaklandathletics.com

SEATTLE MARINERS
SAFECO FIELD
P.O. Box 4100
Seattle, WA 98104
Phone: (206) 346-4000
www.mariners.com

TAMPA BAY DEVIL RAYS
TROPICANA FIELD
One Tropicana Drive
St. Petersburg, FL 33705
Phone: (888) 326-7297
www.devilray.com

TEXAS RANGERS
AMERIQUEST FIELD IN ARLINGTON
1000 Ballpark Way
Arlington, TX 76011
Phone: (817) 273-5222
www.texasrangers.com

TORONTO BLUE JAYS
SKYDOME
One Blue Jays Way, Suite 3200
Toronto, ON M5V1J1, Canada
Phone: (416) 341-1000
www.bluejays.ca

National League

ARIZONA DIAMONDBACKS
Bank One Ballpark
401 East Jefferson Street
Pheonix, AZ 85004
Phone: (602) 462-6000
www.azdiamondbacks.com

ATLANTA BRAVES
Turner Field
755 Hank Aaron Drive
Atlanta, GA 30315
Phone: (404) 522-7630
www.atlantabraves.com

CHICAGO CUBS
Wrigley Field
1060 West Addison
Chicago, IL 60613-4397
Phone: (773) 404-2827
www.cubs.com

CINCINNATI REDS
Great American Ball Park
100 Main Street
Cincinnati, OH 45202
Phone: (513) 765-7000
www.cincinnatireds.com

COLORADO ROCKIES
Coors Field
2001 Blake Street
Denver, CO 80205-2000
Phone: (303) 292-0200
www.coloradorockies.com

FLORIDA MARLINS
Pro Player Stadium
2267 N.W. 199th Street
Miami, FL 33056
Phone: (305) 626-7400
www.flamarlins.com

HOUSTON ASTROS
Minute Maid Field
P.O. Box 288
Houston, TX 77001-0288
Phone: (713) 259-8000
www.astros.com

LOS ANGELES DODGERS
Dodger Stadium
1000 Elysian Park Avenue
Los Angeles, CA 90012-1199
Phone: (323) 244-1500
www.dodgers.com

MILWAUKEE BREWERS
Miller Park
One Brewers Way
Milwaukee, WI 53214-3652
Phone: (414) 902-4000
www.milwaukeebrewers.com

NEW YORK METS
Shea Stadium
123-01 Roosevelt Avenue
Flushing, NY 11368
Phone: (718) 507-METS
www.mets.com

PHILADELPHIA PHILLIES
Citizens Bank Park
One Citizens Bank Way
Philadelphia, PA 19148-5249
Phone: (215) 463-6000
www.phillies.com

PITTSBURGH PIRATES
PNC Park
115 Federal Street
Pittsburgh, PA 15212
Phone: (412) 323-5000
www.pirateball.com

ST. LOUIS CARDINALS
Busch Stadium
250 Stadium Plaza
St. Louis, MO 63102
Phone: (314) 421-3060
www.stlcardinals.com

SAN DIEGO PADRES
PETCO Park
100 Park Blvd.
San Diego, CA 92101
Phone: (619) 795-5000
www.padtes.com

SAN FANCISCO GIANTS
SBC Park
24 Willlie Mays Plaza
San Francisco, CA 94107
Phone: (415) 972-2000
www.sfgiants.com

WASHINGTON NATIONALS
RFK Stadium
2400 East Capitol Street, SE
Washington, D.C. 20003
Phone: (202) 349-0400
www.nationals.com

72-page Eyewitness Titles

American Revolution
Ancient Egypt
Ancient Greece
Ancient Rome
Arms & Armor
Astronomy
Baseball
Basketball
Bird
Castle
Cat
Crystal & Gem
Dance
Dinosaur
Dog
Early Humans
Earth
Explorer
Fish
Flying Machine
Food
Fossil
Future
Horse

Human Body
Hurricane & Tornado
Insect
Islam
Invention
Jungle
Knight
Mammal
Mars
Medieval Life
Mummy
Music
Mythology
NASCAR
North American Indian
Ocean
Olympics
Photography
Pirate
Plant

Pond & River
Pyramid
Religion
Rocks & Minerals
Seashore
Shakespeare
Shark
Shipwreck
Skeleton
Soccer
Space Exploration
Titanic
Tree
Vietnam
Viking
Volcano & Earthquake
Weather
Whale
Wild West
World War I
World War II

Other Eyewitness Titles

Index

Acknowledgments

The author, the publisher, and the Shoreline Publishing Group offer their grateful thanks for assistance in creating this book to: Rick Pilling and Paul Cunningham of Major League Baseball; W.C. Burdick of the National Baseball Hall of Fame and Library; Bob and Ed Rosato of Rosato Sports Photography; Elizabeth Daws of the Rawlings Co.; Hillerick & Bradsby; Carolyn McMahon of AP/World Wide Photos; and the marvelous memorabilia collection of David Spindel.

Special thanks to Bill Pintard of the California state champion Santa Barbara Foresters for helping to arrange for players Adam Berry and Wade Clark to pose for photographs. Additional production assistance was provided by Seth Mandelbaum.

The following books were resources for the author. Note that all statistics in the book are current through October, 2004.

Total Baseball (Total Sports, 1999) by John Thorn, et al. This is the official encyclopedia of Major League Baseball and was the checking source for statistics.
The New Dickinson Baseball Dictionary (Harcourt Brace, 1999) by Paul Dickson
Green Cathedrals (Addison Wesley, 1992) by Philip J. Lowry
The Series (Sporting News, 1991)

Photography Credits:
t = top; b = bottom; l = left;
r = right; c = center

Associated Press 10tl, 10bc, 11c, 11cr, 11cr, 11bc, 11br, 13tl, 20c, 25bl, 25br, 27br, 29tr, 30bl, 30bc, 30br, 30tr, 33br, 34bl, 34br, 35tr, 35cr, 35br, 38-39 (7), 40bl, 40c, 41br, 42cr, 43tl, 43tr, 44bl, 44tr, 45tr, 47tl, 48bl, 48c, 49br, 49tl, 51tr, 52-53 (7), 54bl, 54tr, 55tr, 56tl, 56br, 59tl, 61tl
Michael Burr 16c (5), 16b, 16t, 17c (2), 21br, 24tl (5), 25t (7), 27l, 27cr, 30tl (5),

34cr, 40tl, 43bl, 51bc.
Christie's 36tr.
DK Publishing 14tl.
Scott Cunningham/MLB Photos 63tr.
Mike Eliason 12cr, 14br, 15tl, 17bl, 18c, 20bl, 25bc, 26cl, 28br (3), 31br, 32bl, 33bl, 33cr, 42cr, 42bc, 46br.
Franklin Sports, Inc., 31bc.
Getty Images 56-57
Getty Images/Todd Rosenberg 59b
Library of Congress 6bc, 6c, 7br, 9t, 9tr, 17tl, 22bl, 25c, 41br, 55bl.
Rich Pilling/MLB Photos 12tr, 26bl, 28c, 29br, 30bc, 35l, 55cl, 58 c, 58bl ,58-59
Louis DeLuca/MLB Photos 23cr.
John Grieshop/MLB Photos 60l, 61br.
Brad Mangin/MLB Photos 55br, 57bl
Don Smith/MLB Photos 13c, 32.
National Baseball Hall of Fame and Library 6c, 8tl, 8bc, 15tr, 17tr, 21tr, 34tl, 37tl, 44tl, 45cl, 45c, 49bl, 49c, 49tr.
Rawlings Co. 17tl, 18br, 20tr, 23cl, 27tr.
Bob Rosato/MLB Photos 13bl, 14c, 23l, 26tr, 28bl, 31l, 33cl, 46c.
Scott Rovak/MLB Photos 56-57
Santa Barbara Foresters 59tr.
David Spindel 6tl, 7r, 8c, 8bl, 8cr, 9bl, 9cr, 9bl, 9cr, 9tr, 18cl, 18bl, 19tr, 20br,

21bl, 22tr, 22cr, 22br, 25tr, 26cr, 26br, 30tr, 32tl, 33c, 34cl, 36cl (2), 36bl, 37cl, 40bl, 40br, 46tl, 46tr, 46cl, 47tr, 47br, 50tl, 50bl, 50bc, 50tr, 50cr, 50br, 51tl, 51bl, 51br, 54c, 55tl.
Transcendental Graphics 56tr.
University of Notre Dame Libraries, 45tl, 45br.
Ron Vesely/MLB Photos 12bl; 13bl, 62-63
Wilson Sporting Goods Co., 19c(3).
John Williamson/MLB Photos 62tl.
Michael Zagaris/MLB Photos 57tr.

Jacket credits: *Front:* tl: Courtesy Intergold; tcl: Transcendental Graphics; cl: Wilson Sporting Goods Co.; tcr: Courtesy of Major League Baseball; tr: DK Photo from the collection of James Buckley, Jr.; main image: Joe Skipper/Reuters/Corbis. *Back:* cla: National Baseball Hall of Fame and Library; clb: Rawlings; cra: Wilson Sporting Goods Co.; cr: Michael Burr; crb: National Baseball Hall of Fame and Library; br: Michael Burr.